Technical Textiles

The Authors

D Gopalakrishnan is an M.Tech (Textile Chemistry), M.Sc (Costume Design & Fashion) and MBA (Technology Management) qualified Textile Technologist. He currently pursues his PhD in Textile Technology at Anna University, Chennai. Now he is working as Project staff at Department of Fashion Technology, PSG College of Technology, Coimbatore. He has presented many papers & posters in various national & International conferences. 6 innovative projects in technical textiles and also has several technical articles published in national, international journals & Textile magazines to his credit. He has delivered special lectures and guest lectures in various programmes conducted by other colleges/universities. He has published five books.

Prof. P Vinayagamurthi is the Head of Department of Costume Design and Fashion at Sri Jayendra Saraswathy maha Vidhyalaya College of arts and science, Coimbatore. He has spent over 24 years in industrial experience includes garment pattern development and industrial engineering. He also has 12 years of experience in Academic. He currently pursues his PhD in Textile Technology at Bharathiar University, Coimbatore. He has published 5 articles in National and 2 in International Journals to his credit and has presented 5 papers in National and 2 in International Conferences. He has delivered special lectures and conducted various Faculty development programmes. He has organized and conducted international conference and many workshops.

Technical Textiles

Authors:
D Gopalakrishnan
P Vinayagamurthi

2019
Daya Publishing House®
A Division of
Astral International Pvt. Ltd.
New Delhi – 110 002

Published by   : **Daya Publishing House®**
                           A Division of
                           Astral International Pvt. Ltd.
                           – ISO 9001:2015 Certified Company –
                           4736/23, Ansari Road, Darya Ganj
                           New Delhi-110 002
                           Ph. 011-43549197, 23278134
                           E-mail: info@astralint.com
                           Website: www.astralint.com

Digitally Printed at   : **Replika Press Pvt. Ltd.**

Preface

India currently consumes the products under all twelve categories, though not all of them are produced domestically. The per centage of indigenous production varies drastically across various products. India is a large producer of technical textiles products in Packtech, Clothtech, Hometech and Sportech segments, the products of which are primarily commodities. Unlike the conventional textile industry in India which is highly export intensive, the technical textile industry is an import intensive industry.

The present book is divided into eight chapters. The first chapter is introductory in nature; it gives a synoptic view of the entire technical textile. The second chapter studies the overview of finishing techniques followed for Technical Textiles products and its developments. The third chapter explores the overview of protective and geotextiles. Depicting the description of protective and geotextiles products, the chapter includes application, raw materials and technologies used for the protech products. In fourth chapter, the analysis of growth and development of meditech industry have been explained in terms of production, raw materials and its applications with their performance overviews. The fifth chapter chapter examines the trend in smart textiles during the application and depicts the smart products in various fields. The sixth chapter gives the agriculture; horticulture area has realized the need of tomorrow and opting for various materials and technologies. The seventh chapter offered to promote the automotive textiles, there are few product behind the growth of automotive textiles. The eighth chapter is industrial fabrics that are used for various industrial applications especially view of the filtration textile.

This book is an effort which goes into the basic technical and deep application details as regards technical textiles as well as Textiles in beginner level perspective. It will be of immense help to the students, researchers and young entrepreneurs who are developing new insights into the technical textiles industry. This would certainly contribute to the existing stock of knowledge on the subject matter.

D. Gopalakrishnan

Prof. P. Vinayagamurthi

Coimbatore, Tamilnadu, INDIA

Contents

1

Introduction of Technical Textiles

Technical textiles represent a multi-disciplinary field with numerous end use applications. Depending on the product characteristics, functional requirements and end-use applications, the technical textile products have been broadly grouped into 12 sectors. Each of the 12 group covers number of products and in all there will be hundreds of products. The committee decided to shortlist potential products based on the industry's capability, infra structure, market potential for initial prioritization for development instead of thinly spreading resources on creating support infrastructure for a large number of products.

Major Segments of Technical Textiles

The technical textile is broadly grouped under the following 12 segments based on the functional applicability.

1. Agrotech (agriculture, horticulture and forestry)
2. Buildtech (building and construction)
3. Cloth tech (technical components of shoes and clothing)
4. Geotech (geotextiles, civil engineering)
5. Hometech (components of furniture, household textiles and floor coverings)
6. Indutech (filtration, cleaning and other industrial)
7. Medtech (hygiene and medical)
8. Mobiltech (automobiles, shipping, railways and aerospace)
9. Oekotech(environmental protection)
10. Pactech(packaging)
11. Protech (personal and property protection)
12. Sportech (sport and leisure)

Basic Requirements of Technical Textiles

The traditional textiles are becoming more and more competitive and will have to face tough competition in exports from China and asian countries. Obviously many companies producing traditional textiles have to continuously struggle to survive in a highly competitive global market. In these circumstances, textile manufacturers need to consider some emerging factors and redefine their strategies for production and marketing. Technical textile markets are usually more application specific and demanding altogether different types of production strategies. The strict adherence to the product specification and quality standards are the prime requirements to enter in this field. Usually, there is a need for special dialogue between the producers and the users. The user needs products with specific performance and functional requirement. Therefore, the producers must peep into requirements and translate the same in the products to the satisfaction of the users.

Technical Textiles Classification

According to the end use, technical textiles can be divided into different categories.

Agro tech: These are the Agro-textiles, also known as Agrotex, that are used in agricultural applications related to growing and harvesting of crops and animals. Not only crop production, they are also used in forestry, horticulture, as well as animal and poultry rearing including animal clothing. Agro-textiles have to be strong, elongated, stiff, bio-degradable, resistant to sunlight and toxic environment.

Build tech: These are the Construction Textiles, also known as Build tex, used in construction and architectural applications, such as for concrete reinforcement, facade foundation, interior construction, insulation, air conditioning, noise prevention, visual protection, protection against sun light, building safety etc. The field of textile architecture is also expanding as textile membranes are increasingly being used for roof construction. Such fabrics as PVC coated high tenacity PES, teflon coated glass fiber fabrics or silicone coated PES are used extensively in football stadia, airports and hotels.

Cloth tech: These are the Clothing textiles, also known as Cloth tex, including all those textile products that represent functional, most often hidden components, of clothing and footwear such as interlinings, sewing thread, insulating fibre fill and waddings. They are the 'high performance' garment fabrics whose demand is increasingly rising with the time.

Geo tech: These are the Geo textiles, also known as Geotex, which are woven, nonwoven and knit fabric used for many functions such as support, drainage and separation at or below ground level. Their application areas include civil and coastal engineering, earth and road construction, dam engineering, soil sealing and in drainage systems. Geo tech has good strength, durability, low moisture absorption and thickness. Synthetic fibers such as glass fiber, polypropylene and acrylic fibers are used to prevent cracking of the concrete, plastic and other building materials.

Home tech: These are the Domestic Textiles, also known as Home tex, used in making of many home furnishing fabrics including carpet backings, curtains, wall coverings, etc. They are mostly fire retardant fabrics whose properties are derived either by using fire retardant fibers such as modacrylic fiber or by coating the fabrics with fire retardant additives such as bromide of phosphorus compounds.

Indutech: These are the Industrial Textiles, also known as Indutex, used in different ways by many industries for activities such as separating and purifying industrial products, cleaning gases and effluents, transporting materials between processes and acting as substrates for abrasive sheets and other coated products. They range from lightweight nonwoven filters, knitted nets and brushes to heavyweight coated conveyor belts.

Medtech: These are the Medical Textiles, also known as Medtex. They include all the medical fabrics that are used in health and hygiene applications in both consumer and medical markets. They are generally used in bandages and sutures that are used for stitching the wounds. Sutures and wound dressing uses fibers like silk fibers and other synthetic fibers. Hollow synthetic fibers are used with nano particles (very small particles) for delivery of drugs to any specific part of the body. Cotton, silk, polyester, polyamide fabrics are also used in medical applications.

Mobiltech: These textiles, also known as Mobiltex, are used in transport industry, such as in construction of automobiles, railways, ships etc. Truck covers and restraints are significant textile end-uses in the transportation sector. They can range from simple ropes and tarpaulins to highly engineered flexible curtain systems and webbing tie-downs. Other examples include seat covers, seat belts, non-wovens for cabin air filtration, airbags, parachutes, inflatable boats, air balloons am

Oekotech: These are the Eco-friendly Textiles, also known as Oekotex or Ecotex. They are mostly used in environmental protection applications - floor sealing, erosion protection, air cleaning, prevention of water pollution, water cleaning, waste treatment/recycling, depositing area construction, product extraction, domestic water sewerage plants. They are even gaining unimaginable popularity in other sectors of textile industry. Clothing, home furnishings, fashion accessories etc. all now come in eco-friendly versions made of oekotech.

Packtech: These are the Packaging Textiles, also known as Packtex. Textiles have been used for packaging since ages. It ranges from heavyweight woven fabrics used for bags, packaging sacks, Flexible Intermediate Bulk Carriers (FIBCs) and wrappings for textile bales and carpets to the lightweight nonwovens used as durable papers, tea bags and other food and industrial product wrappings.

Protech: These are the Protective Textiles, also known as Protex, that are used in the manufacturing of protective clothing of different types. Protection against heat and radiation for fire fighter clothing, against molten metals for welders, for bullet proof jackets or for chemical protective clothing- all depend on the use of protech. The protective textiles are made with the help of specialty fibers such as aramid fiber used in making of bullet proof jackets, glass fibers used in fire proof jackets etc. Sometimes the protective textile is also coated with special chemicals, for example, when used in manufacturing astronauts suits.

Sporttech: These are the Sports Textiles, also known as Sporttex, used mainly for making sports wear including sports shoes and other sports accessories. Increasing interest in active sports and outdoor leisure activities such as flying and sailing sports, climbing, cycling, etc. has led to immense growth in the consumption of textile materials in manufacturing sporting and related goods and equipment. Synthetic fibers and coatings have largely replaced traditional cotton fabrics and other natural fibers in the making of spottech.

Applications of Technical textiles

Agriculture, Horticulture and Fishing

Textiles have always been used extensively in the course of food production, most notably by the fishing industry in the form of nets, ropes and lines but also by agriculture and horticulture for a variety of covering, protection and containment applications. Although future volume growth rates appear to be relatively modest, this is partly due to the replacement of heavier weight traditional textiles, including jute and sisal sacking and twine, by lighter, longer lasting synthetic substitutes, especially polypropylene. Lightweight spun bonded fleeces are now used for shading, thermal insulation and weed suppression. Heavier nonwoven, knitted and woven constructions are employed for wind and hail protection. Fibrillated and extruded nets are replacing traditional baler twine for wrapping modern circular bales. Capillary nonwoven matting is used in horticulture to distribute moisture to growing plants. The bulk storage and transport of fertilizer and agricultural products is increasingly undertaken using woven polypropylene FIBCs (flexible intermediate bulk containers blister and big bags) in place of jute, paper or plastic sacks. At sea, fish farming is a growing industry which uses specialized netting and other textile products. High performance fibres such as HMPE (e.g. Dyneema and Spectra) are finding their way into the fishing industry for the manufacture of lightweight, ultra-strong lines and nets.

Construction-building and Roofing

Textiles are employed in many ways in the construction of buildings, both permanent and temporary, dams, bridges, tunnels and roads. A closely related but distinct area of use is in geo-textiles by the civil engineering sector. Temporary structures such as tents, marquees and awnings are some of the most obvious and visible applications of textiles where these used to be exclusively made from proofed heavy cotton, a variety of lighter, stronger, rot, sunlight and weatherproof synthetic materials are now increasingly required. Nonwoven glass and polyester fabrics are already widely used in roofing applications while other textiles are used as breathable membranes to prevent moisture penetration of walls. Fibres and textiles also have a major role to play in building and equipment insulation. Glass fibres are almost universally used in place of asbestos now. Double wall spacer fabrics can be filled with suitable materials to provide sound and thermal insulation or serve as lightweight cores for composite materials. Composites generally have a bright future in building and construction. Existing applications of glass-reinforced materials include wall panels, septic tanks and sanitary fittings. Glass, polypropylene and acrylic fibres and textiles are all used to prevent cracking of concrete, plaster and other building materials. More innovative use is now being made of glass in bridge construction.

Home Textiles

By far the largest area of use for other textiles as defined above, that is other than fabrics, nonwovens and composite reinforcements, over 35% of the total weight of fibres and textiles in that category, lies in the field of household textiles and furnishing and especially in the use of loose fibres in wadding and fiberfill applications. Hollow fibres with excellent insulating properties are widely used in bedding and sleeping bags. Other types of fibre are increasingly being used to replace foams in furniture because of concern over the fire and health hazards posed by such materials. Woven fabrics are still used to a significant extent as carpet and furniture backings and in some smaller, more specialized areas such as curtain header tapes. However, nonwovens such as spun bonded have made significant inroads into these larger markets while various dry laid and hydro-entangled products are now widely used in household cleaning applications in place of traditional mops and dusters.

Medical and Hygiene Textiles

The largest use of textiles is for hygiene applications such as wipes, babies' diapers and adult sanitary and incontinence products. Nonwovens dominate these applications which account for over 23% of all nonwoven use, the largest proportion of any of the 12 major markets for technical textiles. The other side of the medical and hygiene market is a rather smaller but higher value market for medical and surgical products such as operating gowns and drapes, sterilization packs, dressings, sutures and orthopaedic pads. At the highest value end of this segment are relatively tiny volumes of extremely sophisticated textiles for uses such as artificial ligaments, veins and arteries, skin replacement, hollow fibres for dialysis machines and so on.

Geo-textiles in Civil Engineering

The economic and environmental advantages of using textiles to reinforce, stabilise, separate, drain and filter are already well proven. Geotextiles allow the building of railway and road cuttings and embankments with steeper sides, reducing the land required and disturbance to the local environment. Revegetation of these embankments or of the banks of rivers and waterways can also be promoted using appropriate materials.

Transportation Textiles

Transport applications (cars, Lorries, buses, trains, ships and aerospace) represent the largest single end-use area for technical textiles, accounting for some 20% of the total. Products range from carpeting and seating (regarded as technical rather than furnishing textiles because of the very stringent performance characteristics which they must fulfil), through tyre, belt and hose reinforcement, safety belts and air bags, to composite reinforcements for automotive bodies, civil and military aircraft bodies, wings and engine components, and many other uses.

Packaging and Containment

Important uses of textiles include the manufacturing of bags and sacks, traditionally. An even faster growing segment of the packaging market uses lighter weight nonwovens and knitted structures for a variety of wrapping and protection applications, especially in the food industry. Tea and coffee bags use wet-laid nonwovens. Meats, vegetables and fruits are now frequently packed with a nonwovens insert to absorb liquids. Other fruits and vegetable products are supplied in knitted net packaging from cotton, flax and jute but increasingly from polypropylene. Strong, lightweight spun bonded and equivalent nonwoven paper-like materials are particularly useful for courier envelopes while adhesive tapes, often reinforced with fibres, yarns and fabrics, are increasingly used in place of traditional twine. Woven strapping are less dangerous to cut than the metal bands and wires traditionally used with densely packed bales.

Protective and Safety Clothing and Textiles

Textiles for protective clothing and other related applications are another important growth area which has attracted attention and interest somewhat out of proportion to the size and value of the existing market. The variety of protective functions that needs to be provided by different textile products is considerable and diverse. It includes protection against cuts, abrasion, ballistic and other types of severe impact including stab wounds and explosions, fire and extreme heat, hazardous dust and particles, nuclear, biological and chemical hazards, high voltages and static electricity, foul weather, extreme cold and poor visibility.

Sports Textiles

Applications are diverse and range from artificial turf used in sports surfaces through to advanced carbon fibre composites for racquet frames, fishing rods, golf clubs and cycle frames. Other highly visible uses are balloon fabrics, parachute and paraglide fabrics and sailcloth.

Ecological Protection Textiles

The final category of technical textile markets, as defined by Techtextil, is technical textiles for protection of the environment and ecology. This is not a well defined segment yet, although it overlaps with several other areas, including industrial textiles (filtration media), geotextiles (erosion protection and sealing of toxic waste) and agricultural textiles (e.g. minimizing water loss from the land and reducing the need for use of herbicides by providing mulch to plants).

Domestic Scenario of Technical Textiles in India

India currently consumes the products under all 12 categories of technical textiles, though not all of them are produced domestically. The per centage of indigenous production varies drastically across various products. India is a large producer of products in Packtech, Clothtech, Hometech and Sportech segments of technical textiles. The products with high production levels in India and with substantial exports are typically commodities and are not very R&D intensive such as flexible intermediate bulk containers (FIBCs), tarpaulins, jute carpet backing, hessian, fishnets, surgical dressings, crop covers, etc. Unlike the conventional textile industry in India which is highly export intensive, the technical textile industry is an import intensive industry. Many products like baby diapers, adult diapers, polypropylene spunbond fabric for disposables, wipes, protective clothing, hoses, webbings for seat belts, etc. are imported to a very large extent. Size of the units manufacturing technical textile products also varies to a large extent. There are some large domestic players in this industry like SRF, Entremonde Polycoaters, Kusumgarh Corporates, Supreme Nonwovens Pvt. Ltd., Garware Wall Ropes, Century Enka, Techfab India Ltd., Ahlstrom, Pacific Non Woven, Vardhman, Unimin, etc. In addition, there are a few Multi National large players in technical textiles like Johnson & Johnson, Du Pont, Procter & Gamble, 3M, SKAPs, Kimberly Clark, etc. who have set up their manufacturing facilities in India. Although there are various large players in this industry, production of certain products is still concentrated in the small scale segment like canvas tarpaulin, carpet backing, woven sacks, shoe laces, soft luggage, zip fasteners, stuffed toys, fabrication of awnings, canopies and blinds, etc. The India Technical Textile Industry is on the threshold of the tidal wave of growth. The India has all ingredients to emerge as a powerhouse of technical textiles (for both commodity as well as high-end products) and the momentum which has been building up for some time is expected to accelerate and would catapult India into the league of major technical textile producers within next 5 years.

Technical textiles that find hygiene and medical applications are termed as medical textiles (Meditech). Key applications include surgical gowns, drapes, sutures, sanitary napkins, diapers, woven, knit, nonwoven wound care and sterile packaging. The Meditech segment was valued close to US$ 12 Bn in 2016 and is expected to be valued at almost US$ 20 Bn by the end of 2026, registering a CAGR of 4.9% over the forecast period. The segment is projected to represent an incremental $ opportunity of more than US$ 7 Bn in 2027 over 2017, mainly contributed by the rising number of applications in surgical equipment, dressings and clothing designed for patient comfort. Technical textiles that find applications in geo-textiles and civil engineering are termed as geo textiles. Key applications include ground stabilization, soil reinforcement, and erosion control. The Geotech segment accounted for a market value of US$ 4 Bn in 2016 and is projected to be valued at close to US$ 7 Bn by 2027. Rising number of applications in the field of civil engineering such as separation and stabilisation, filtration and reinforcement are expected to drive demand for industrial textiles over the forecast period.

Technical textiles that find applications in environmental protection are termed as ecological protection textiles (Oekotech). Key applications include recycling schemes, products for oil spill treatment and erosion control. The Oekotech segment was valued at a little more than US$ 4 Bn in 2016 and is expected to reach a market valuation in excess of US$ 6.5 Bn by the end of 2027, registering a CAGR of 5.1% over the forecast period. Technical textiles that find applications in building and construction are termed as Buildtech. Key applications include wall reinforcements, house wrap, facades, concrete wraps, sewer and pipe, and linings. The Buildtech segment was valued at US$ 13 Bn in 2016 and is estimated to be valued in excess of US$ 22 Bn by the end of 2027, expanding at a CAGR of 5.6% over the forecast period. Medical textile manufacturers have been focusing on refining existing products as well as on new product development to derive new materials with improved designs and features.

Future of the Technical Textiles Industry

The future of technical textiles embraces a much wider economic sphere of activity than just the direct manufacturing and processing of textiles. The industry's suppliers include raw materials producers (both natural and artificial), machinery and equipment manufacturers, information and management technology providers, R&D services, testing and certification bodies, consultants, education and training organizations. The new millennium promises even fiercer international competition which will see manufacturers striving to engineer costs downwards and develop global economies of scale in production and product development. Technical textiles will become better 'value for money' than ever before and this should open the way towards further applications as existing end-uses mature.

2

Finishing of Technical Textiles

Nano finishing is concerned with positive control and processing technologies in the sub nano meter range and so must play an essential role in the fabrication of extremely precise and fine parts. The Nano technology has laid its imprints in all the fields of science and engineering. And the textile industry in not an exception to this. with the immeasurable potential of this technology it is possible to create an entirely new generation of textile products that are cleaner, stronger, lightered and more precise with its multifunctional finishes. The development of ultra fine fibers, functional finishes and smart textiles based on the nano technology has end less properties and their functional properties are more superior than the conventional process due to their higher surface area to volume ratio with their nano finishing. Nano is not a single technology, but a million different things. And its unique feature is that there is some thing small about it with its finishing .It would be appropriate to say that "The Next Big Thing Is Really small". as Nano technology as a whole is still in relatively early stage of development, it is attracting lots of research work and it would not be hyperbole to state "Tiny particles are going to shape our future with its next generation finishing like (nano –care , nano-pel , nano- touch , nano-dry,nano-sphere).

Introduction

Nano finishing means any technology done on a nanometer or (10^{-9}) meter scale. the main aim of the nano finishing is "the precise manipulation of an individual atoms and molecules to create a structure. This technology was launched 40 years ago by Richard Feynmanand. Then next milestone was achieved by publishing K. Eric Drexler's definite book about nanotechnology. The nano technology was adapted to textile in 1998 by Dr. David Soane. It is applicable in producing nanofibres, color changeable cloths, anti-stain, anti-wrinkle and some other finishing processes and also in filter fabrics.

The future of technology at times becomes easier to predict. Computer will Compute faster, materials will become stronger, the technology that works on the nanometer scale. The molecules and atoms will be large part of this future, enabling the textile field of human presence. It is raising wave in textile to get a product which is having high quality and precision.Nanotechnology is much discussed these days as an emerging frontier –a real in which machines operate at a scale of billionths of a meter. It is actually a multitude of rapidly emerging technologies, based upon the scaling down of existing technologies to the next level of precision and miniaturization. Nanotechnology is regarded as the next basic technology to follow IT and Biotechnology.

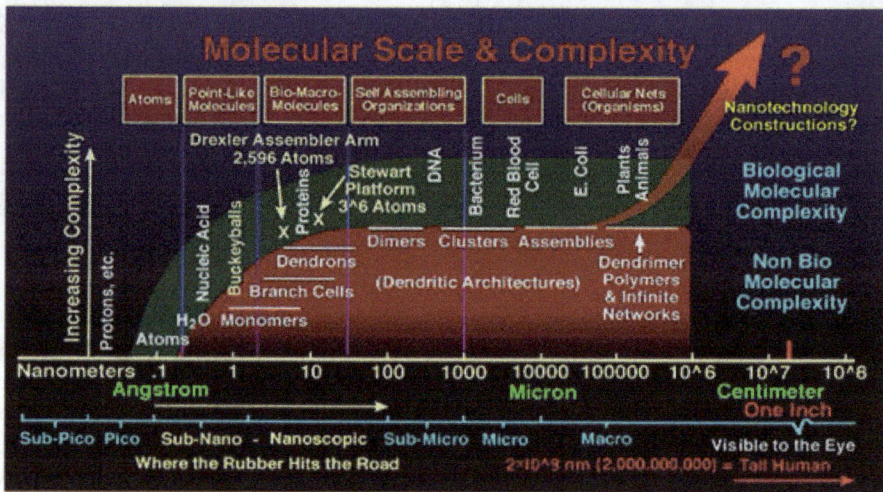

Application of Nano Finishing

Anti Static Performance

Static usually builds up in synthetic fibers such as nylon and polyester because they absorb little water. Cellulosic fibers have higher moisture content to carry away static charges, thus a static charge not accumulate. Conventionally surfactants are used to spread the small amount of moisture on the surface of fiber so as to cause the charge to leak away. Surfactants containing N-methylol compounds can also improve the durability of the fabric. Since N-methylol compounds can chemically bond the surfactants to the fibers.

Nano-Tex

Nano-Tex has begun with applying the technology in readily-available natural fibers such as cotton, wool and silk, as well as synthetics including polyester and nylon. Nano-Tex™ Resists Spills Fabric Protection Repel Ink. Inks and dyes contain concentrated amounts of quick-drying colorants. Fabrics treated with NANO-TEX Resists Spills protection are not protected from these types of colorants but if lifted quickly, stains can be minimized.

NANO-TEX Resists Spills fabric protection protects against both water-based and oil-based liquids. Resists Spills fabric protection offers superior liquid repellency, which helps to minimize stains. If the mud is sitting on the surface of the fabric, NANO-TEX fabric protection will allow the wearer to carefully lift off the mud, therefore minimize staining. If the mud has been ground into the NANO-TEX Resists Spills enhanced fabric, recommended garment care cleaning tips should be followed to minimize or prevent the potential for staining. Mud stains or thick oils that are smeared onto fabric may leave some residual staining.

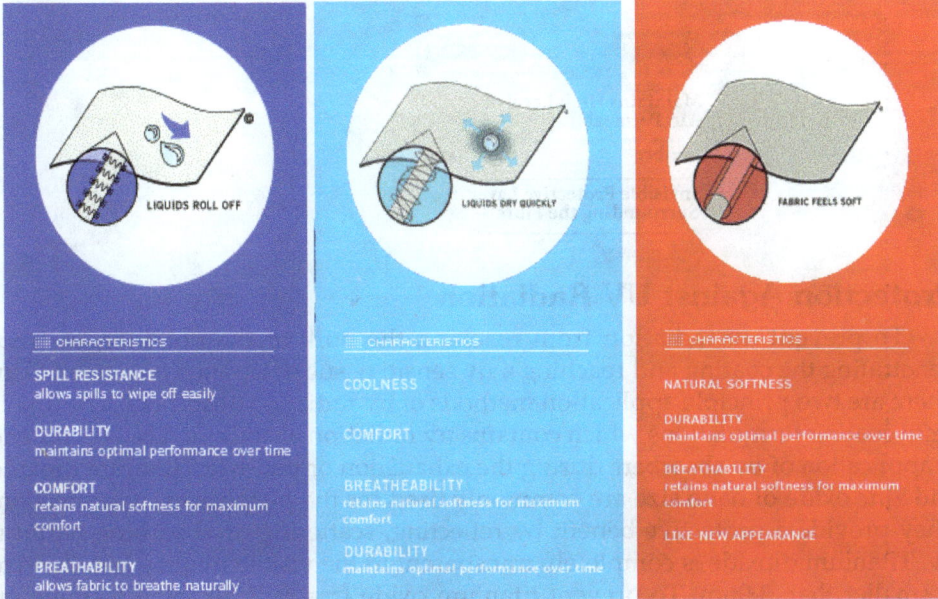

CHARACTERISTICS	CHARACTERISTICS	CHARACTERISTICS
SPILL RESISTANCE allows spills to wipe off easily	COOLNESS	NATURAL SOFTNESS
DURABILITY maintains optimal performance over time	COMFORT	DURABILITY maintains optimal performance over time
COMFORT retains natural softness for maximum comfort	BREATHEABILITY retains natural softness for maximum comfort	BREATHABILITY retains natural softness for maximum comfort
BREATHABILITY allows fabric to breathe naturally	DURABILITY maintains optimal performance over time	LIKE-NEW APPEARANCE

Nano-Tex™ Resists Spills Fabric Protection Resist Mud Stains

Nano Sphere

NanoSphere" from Schoeller Textiles AG got an acknowledgement from Design Prize Switzerland 2001 for Textile Design. The Swiss textile technolgy company's natural water-repellent, dirt-repellent, anti-adhesive and self-cleaning finishing process was awarded for its futuristic development and applications.

"NanoSphere" was inspired by nature and conceived through nano-technology. Certain plant leaves, beetle shells and insect wings always stay clean due to the difficulty that particles of dirt have in sticking to their infinitesimal rough, structured surfaces, letting even the lightest rainfall clean the surface.. By applying "NanoSphere" technology to textiles, a special three-dimensional surface structure is created, limiting the available contact surface for dirt particles. The remaining particles are suspended in drops of water and are easily swept away as the water drops off. It is an impregnating treatment that makes fabrics water and soil resistant. Nano sphere impregnation involves a three dimensional surface structure with gel forming additives which repel water and prevent dirt particles from attaching themselves.

Protects Fabric Against Water & Strain

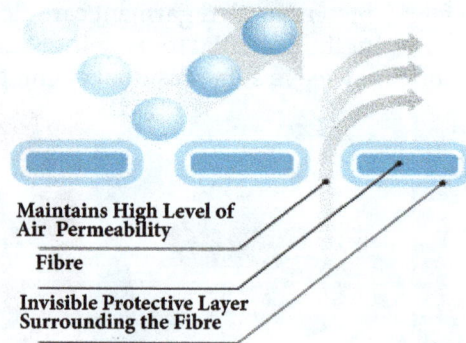

Maintains High Level of
Air Permeability

Fibre

Invisible Protective Layer
Surrounding the Fibre

Protection Against UV Radiation

To prevent uv radiation from reaching the bulk of the polymer, or from penetrating the coating and reaching a uv sensitive substrate such as human skin. There are two principle application methods of uv radiation absorbers. The first is resin coating formulations which contains uv radiation absorbers. The second one is application of uv absorbers during the exhaustion or pad-batcTitanium dioxide and zinc oxide of nano size are commonly used for the purpose of uv protection. They provide a protective benefit by reflecting, scattering or absorbing harmful uv. Titanium dioxide is completely transparent in the visible range when the size is smaller that 300nm. To prevent titanium oxide free radicals from forming on exposure to sunlight, a coating with silica can be applied.

Nanoparticles in Finishing

Nanoparticles such as metal oxides and ceramics are also used in textile finishing to alter surface properties and impart textile functions. Nanosize particles have a larger surface area and hence higher efficiency than larger size particles. Besides, nanosize particles are transparent, and do not blur color and brightness of the textile substrates. However, preventing nanoparticles from aggregation is the key to achieve a desired performance.

As an example, the fabric treated with nanoparticles TiCh and MgO replaces fabrics with active carbon, previously used as chemical and biological protective materials. The photocatalytic activity of TiO_2 and MgO nanoparticles can break harmful and toxic chemicals and biological agents. These nanoparticles can be pre-engineered to adhere to textile substrates by using spray coating or electrostatic methods. Finishing with nanoparticles can convert fabrics into sensor-based materials. If nanocrystalline piezoceramic particles are incorporated into fabrics, the finished fabric can convert exerted mechanical forces into electrical signals enabling the monitoring of bodily functions such as heart rhythm and pulse if they are worn next to ski.

Next Generation Carefree Finishing That Withstands 50 Washes

Nano-Care

A technology that brings about an entirely carefree fabric with wrinkle resistant, shrink proof, water and stain repellent properties, intended for use in cellulosic fibers such as cotton and linen. It is a next-generation, ease-of-care, dimension-stabilizing finish, one step ahead of methods that simply give wrinkle resistance and shrink-proofing. Nano-Care withstands more than 50 home launderings. It imparts water repellency and stain resistance superior to those of conventional methods, maintaining high water and oil repellency levels (80 and 4) even after 20 home washes.

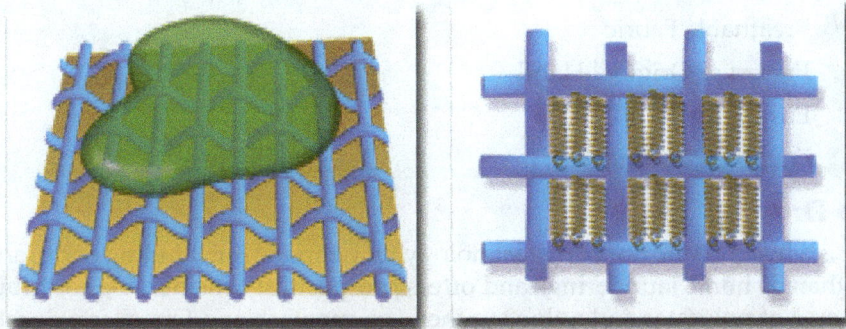

Key Features

- Superior Stain, Water, And Oil Repellency
- Resists Wrinkles
- Breathable Fabric
- Preserves Original Hand
- Easy Care

Nano-Pel

BEFORE   **AFTER**

This nanotech application of water-and-oil repellent finishing is effective for use in natural fibers such as cotton, linen, wool and silk, as well as synthetics such as polyester, nylon and acryl. Unsurpassed performance in durability and water and oil repellency may be expected particularly with natural fibers. Nano-Pel cotton withstands 50 home launderings, with functionality levels well-maintained for water and oil repellency (80 and 4) even after 20 washes

Key Features

- Superior Water and Oil Repellency
- Minimize Stains
- Breathable Fabric
- Preserves Original Hand
- Easy Care
- Durable Performance

Nano-Dry

It is a hydrophilic finishing technology that imparts outstanding endurance of more than 50 home launderings and offers prospects of considerable contribution to the area of polyester and nylon synthetic garments. Nano-Dry exerts durability superior to that of the hydrophilic finishing of polyester commonly carried out in Japan using polyethylene glycol polymer molecules, and allows no dye migration when deep-dyed. It is expected to serve particularly well for use in nylon, as there exists no such durable hydrophilic finishing, in the field of sportswear and underwear that require perspiration absorbency. Considerable growth is expected within the forthcoming period of 3 to 6 months, mainly in the field of sportswear.

Key Features

- Moisture Wicking
- Retains Breathability of Fabric
- Quick Drying
- Preserves Original Hand
- Durable Performance

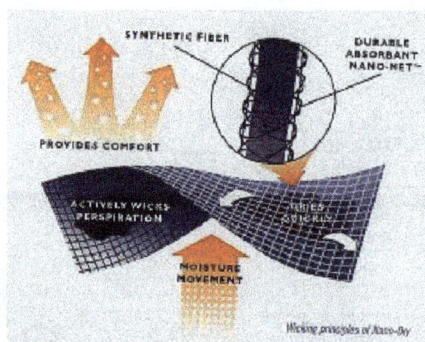

Nano-Touch

This ultimate finishing technology gives a durable cellulose wrapping over synthetic fiber. Cellulosic sheath and synthetic core together form a concentric structure to bring overall solutions to the disadvantages of synthetics being hydrophobic, electrostatic, having artificial hand and glaring luster. It will broaden the existing use of synthetics, being free of their disadvantages as found in synthetic suits being hydrophobic, electrostatic and having unnatural hand. The following are examples of new areas of use created through Nano-Touch, a new standard for fiber compounding.

Self-assembled nanolayer (SAN) coating is a challenge to traditional textile coating. Research in this area is still in embryo stage. In self-assembled nanolayer (SAN) coating, target chemical molecules form a layer of thickness less than nanometer on the surface of textile materials. Additional layers can be added on the top of the existing ones creating a nanolayered structure. Different SAN approaches are being explored to confer special functions to textile materials.

Key Features

- Superior Refinement in a Blended Fabric
- Durable Performance
- Luxurious Cotton-Like Hand
- Easy Care
- Reduced Static Build-up

The self-assembly process begins by exposing a charged surface to a solution of an oppositely charged polyelectrolyte. The amount of adsorbed material is self-limiting by the charge density of the substrate[21]. Surplus polymer solution adhering to the support is removed by simply washing it in a neutral solution. Under the proper conditions, the polyion is adsorbed with more than the stoichiometric number of charges relative to the substrate, reversing the sign of the surface charge. In consequence, when the substrate is exposed to a second solution containing a polyion of opposite charge, an additional polyion layer is adsorbed reversing in this way the sign of the surface charge once again. Consecutive cycles with alternating adsorption of polyanions and polycations result in step-wise growth in total thickness of polymer films.

The fundamentals of the electrostatic self-assembly are more complicated than they appeared to be. " Although this technique is based on the electrostatic attraction between positively and negatively charged species, the interaction between these charged species is specific to the nature of the substrate and that of the polyclectrolytes.

Finish Easy Care - Hydrophobic Nano

Hydrophobic surfaces can be produced mainly in two ways:

1) By creating a rough structure on a hydrophobic surface

2) By modifying a rough surface using materials with low surface free energy.

Both these approaches have been used to give a hydrophobic finish to textile substrates. Fluorocarbon finishes constitute an important class of hydrophobic finishes. These finishes first applied to textiles in the 1960s to impart water and oil repellency have shown considerable growth during last decade. Fluorocarbons are a class of organic chemicals that contain a perfluoroalkyl residue in which all the hydrogen atoms have been replaced by fluorine. These chemicals have been replaced by fluorine and have very high thermal stability and low reactivity. They considerably reduce the surface tension. The critical surface tension (γ_c) of -CF_3 is 6 N m^{-1}. Fluorocarbon finishes are dispersions of per fluorinated acrylates having comonomers. The structure of the fluorinated acrylates can be chemically engineered by varying the proportion of hydrophobic and hydrophilic groups in the side chains to produce specific properties. Durable fluorocarbon finishes have reactive methanol or epoxy groups that may react to form a cross-linked network that may also get covalently bonded to the surface of the fibres. These finishes form low energy films that protect the fibres in the treated fabrics.

Super Hydrophobic - Biomimatic Self Cleaning - Lotus Effect

Hydrophobias fluorocarbon finishes as discussed above lower the surface energy and can give a maximum water contact angle of roughly 120°. To get maximum contact angles and to have self-cleaning ability, super-hydrophobic finish with a contact angle of above 150° is required. The increase in surface roughness provides a large geometric area for a relatively small projected area. The roughened surface generally takes the form of a substrate member with a multiplicity of microscale to nanoscale projections or cavities. The investigators analyzed the surface characteristics by high-resolution SEM and measured the contact angle (CA) of leaves from 340 plant species. The majority of the wettable leaves (CA < 110°) investigated were more or less smooth without any prominent surface sculpturing. In particular, epicuticular wax crystals were absent. In contrast, water-repellent leaves exhibited various surface sculptures mainly epicuticular wax crystals in combination with papillose epidermal cells. Their CAs always exceeded 150°. They observed that on water-repellent surfaces, water contracted to form spherical droplets. It came off the leaf very quickly, even at slight angles of inclination (< 5°), without leaving any residue. Particles of all kind that were adhering to the leaf surface were always removed entirely from water-repellent leaves when subjected to natural or artificial rain, as long as the surface waxes were not destroyed.

Lotus Effect

The dirt particles deposited on the waxy surface of the leaves are generally larger than the microstructure of the surface of the leaf and are hence deposited on the tips; as a result the interfacial area between both is minimized. In the case of a water droplet rolling over a particle, the surface area of the droplet exposed to air is reduced and energy through adsorption is gained. Since the adhesion between particle and surface is greater than the adhesion between particle and water droplet, the particle is 'captured' by the water droplet and removed from the leaf surface. This phenomenon is called 'Lotus Effect', could be impressively demonstrated with sacred lotus (*Nelumbo nucifera*).

Photo Catalytic Self-Cleaning

During the last two decades, advanced orientation processes that are combination of powerful oxidizing agents (catalytic initiators) with UV or near – UV light have been applied for the removal of organic pollutants and xenobiotics from textile effluents among them, TiO_2 has been proved to be an excellent catalyst in the photo degradation of colorants and other organic pollutants. Photo catalytic propensity of semi conductors such as TiO_2 has been attributed the valence band to the conduction band brought above by the absorption of a photon of ultra-band gap light. In the coating composition developed by XIN and Daoud, a sol mixture may be prepared at Room temp by mixing titanium tetraisopropoxide, ethanol and acetic acid in a molar ratio of 1:100:0.05 respectively.

The fabric to be coated was dried at 100⁰C for 30 min, dipped in the above mentioned nanosol for 30sec and then pressed at a nip pressure of 2.75 kg/cm² .The pressed substrates were then dried then at 80⁰C for 10 min in a pre-heated oven to drive off ethanol and finally cured at 100⁰C for 5 min in a pre-heated curing oven. Nano sized TiO_2 particles show high photo catalytic activities because they have a large surface area per unit mass and volume as well as diffusion of the electron/ holes before recombination. This finish also have anti bacterial properties after having been subject to 55 washes through home laundry machine & UV protection characteristics for 20 washes.

Flame Retardant Finish

Nyacol nano technologies, Inc has been the world's leading supplier of colloidal antimony pentoxide which is used for flame retardant finish in textile. It offers colloidal antimony pentoxide us fine particle dispersion for use as a flame retardant synergist with halogenated flame-retardants. (The ratio of halogen to antimony is 5:1 to 2:1). Nano antimony pentoxide used with Halogenated flame-retardants for a flame retardant finishes. 10 parts of nycal in 1550 parts of aqueous dispersion, with pH 7 and add 40 parts of H_2O and sufficient ammonia add for bring out pH 9, mix this with 50 parts of rubber latex and spray to the Non-woven material.

UV-Protection

Previously organic and in organic UV absorbers were coated on the textile material they prevent UV radiation effectively but they are less durable.UV blockers are usually certain semiconductor oxides such as TiO_2, ZnO, SiO_2 and Al_2O_3. Among these semiconductor oxides, titanium dioxide (TiO_2) and zinc oxide (ZnO) are commonly used. It was determined that nano-sized titanium dioxide and zinc oxide were more efficient at absorbing and scattering UV radiation than the conventional size and were thus better able to block UV . This is due to the fact that nano-particles have a larger surface area per unit mass and volume than the conventional materials, leading to the increase of the effectiveness of blocking UV radiation. For small particles, light scattering predominates at approximately one-tenth of the wavelength of the scattered light. Rayleigh's scattering theory stated that the scattering was strongly dependent upon the wavelength, where the scattering was inversely proportional to the wavelength to the fourth power. This theory predicts that in order to scatter UV radiation between 200 and 400 nm, the optimum particle size will be between 20 and 40 nm . UV-blocking treatment for cotton fabrics was developed using the sol-gel method. A thin layer of titanium dioxide is formed on the surface of the treated cotton fabric which provides excellent UV-protection; the effect can be maintained after 50 home launderings . Apart from water droplet rolls titanium dioxide, zinc oxide nanorods of 10 to 50 nm in length were applied to cotton fabric to provide UV protection . According to the study of the UV-blocking effect, the fabric treated with zinc oxide nanorods demonstrated an excellent UV protective factor (UPF) rating.

Anti-Static Finish

Static charge usually formed during processing synthetic fibers such as nylon and polyester because their moisture content. Cellulose fibre such as cotton have higher moisture content to carry away static charges, so that no static charge will accumulate. As synthetic fibres provide poor anti-static properties,. It was determined that nano-sized titanium dioxide , zinc oxide whiskers, nano antimony-doped tin oxide (ATO) and silane nanosol could impart anti-static properties to synthetic fibres. TiO_2, ZnO and ATO provide anti-static effects because they are electrically conductive materials. Such material helps to effectively dissipate the static charge which is accumulated on the fabric. On the other hand, silane nanosol improves anti-static properties, as the silane gel particles on fibre absorb water and moisture in the air by amino and hydroxyl groups and bound water.

Odour Fights Finish

A Taiwanesse nanotech firm Greensheild has created underwear that fights odour. This is achieved through nanotechnolgy. The underwear fibers release undetectable negative ions and infrared rays that destroy odour-causing bacteria. The negative ions create a magnetic field that inhibits the reproduction of bacteria, thus eliminating odour and lowering the risk of skin infection or irritation. Far infrared rays are absorbed by cells not just in the skin but throughout the body – causing all the individual atoms being vibrated at a higher frequency, which speeds up the metabolism and the elimination of wastes. Tourmaline a natural mineral limits a low-level radiation which in contact with oxygen, carbon di oxide and water molecules in the air promotes electrolytic dissociation and emits negative ions. This Nano finish can eliminate up to 99.99% of bacteria, 90% of odour and 75% sticky moisture within the cloth as well as contributing to the overall health of wearer.

Antimicrobial Finishes

Among the various antimicrobial agents used for the finishing of textile substrates, silver or silver ions have long been known to have strong inhibitory and bacterial effects as well as a broad spectrum of antimicrobial activities. The inhibitory effect of silver ion/silver metal on bacteria has been attributed to the interaction of silver ion with thiol groups in bacteria as well as to the oxidative destruction of microorganism in aqueous medium. Silver ion based antimicrobial finishes have been developed by the interaction of a silver salt such as silver nitrate with anionic copolymer of styrene, ethyl acrylate, acrylic acid and divinyl benzene having at least about 0.008 m eq of carboxyl groups per gram of polymer and [3] 0.0009 m mol of silver per gram of the polymer. The films of such polymeric finishes release antibacterial and anti fungal silver ions slowly over a very long period of time. In another patent, it is disclosed that a silver containing antimicrobial agent that has affinity for textile fibres can be produced by treating cross-linked caroxy methyl cellulose (CMC) having > 0.4 carboxy methyl groups with silver nitrate. The antimicrobial finishing agent may have 0.01-0.1% silver bound to the water resistant cross-linked CMC (Ag).

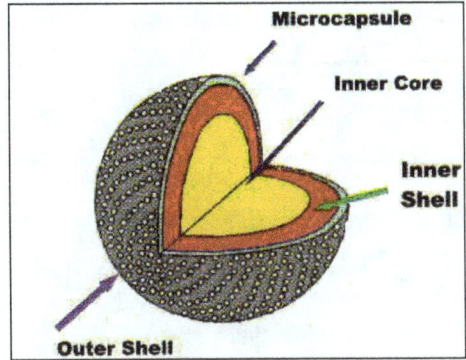

Yang has pattented the a process for preparing a silver nanoparticles containing functional microcapsule having the intrinsic antimicrobial and therapeutic functions of silver as well as additional functional of the products contained in the inner core of the capsule. Such microcapsule can be prepared by a two-step process. In the first step an emulsified solution of a perfume is encapsulated with melanin precondensate. The microcapsule so produced is treated with silver nanoparticle dispersed in water-soluble styrene maleic anhydride polymer solution before it fully dries. Thus microcapsules with duel function are produced. In these microcapsules, the silver nanoparticles are on the surface of the capsule, Instead of a perfume, one can have a thermosensitive pigment, thermal storage material or pharmaceutical preparation in the inner core.

Significant progress has been made in recent years in both design advances, and in tools for the imaging and synthesis of molecular structures. Within the past five years, the pace of development has increased with more efforts specifically focused on developing capabilities to manipulate individual atoms and molecules, and to create structures to atomic specification. There are many important incentives which make it seem likely that the pace of development will continue to grow. Nano technology is a high tech wave that is designing to sweep the world. The probability of the type of commercial applications covered in this topic occurring with in the next few years is quite high. The development of ultra fine fibers, functional finishes and smart textiles based on the nanotechnology has end less properties. At present, the application of nano technology in textiles has merely reaches only the starting line. The reason for less commercilisation of nano technology is due to their higher time consumption and cost factor involved. In future, one can expect to see many more developments in textiles based on nano technology.

3

Protective Textiles

The term "protective textiles" literally means textiles used at the environment is consider to have the highest priority where protection of individual is considered un the defense application such as rain, snow, fog, wind, lighting, sun light, dust and also it should have to survive the intense heat, cold, wetness, UV light, windchill and other discomforts on land, sea and in the air. A market that is receptive to new products and suppliers and abounding with niche markets.

Protective Clothing Compilation

Productive clothing can be divided in to the following groups:

- Clothing against heat and flame
- Clothing against mechanical impacts
- Fire men's protective clothing
- Clothing against cold
- Clothing against foul weather(moisture wind)
- Clothing against chemical substances (gas liquids, particles)
- Clothing against radio active contamination

Extreme Cold

Cold protection requires products with high degrees of insulation, the least bulk, good/relative comfort, and still allowing good dexterity for doing useful work. Still air is a poor conductor of heat, so insulation requires a layer of still air between the skin the source of the heat or cold.

Ballistic Protective Materials

Most military casualties which are due to high speed ballistic projectiles are not caused by bullets. The main threat is from fragmenting devices. In combat, this means in particular grenades, mortars, artillery shells, mines, and improvised explosive devises used by the terrorists. There may also be casualties from the secondary effects of bombs including collapsing buildings, exploding air craft, sinking ships and flying debris. Shield technology lays the parallel strands of synthetic fibres side –by-side and holds them in place with a thermoplastic resin, creating a unidirectional tape. Two layers of the tape are then cross – plied at right angles (0 or 90) and fused in to a composite structure under heat and pressure. The cross plied unidirectional panels are then pre consolidated into rolls, which are used to make the finished products.

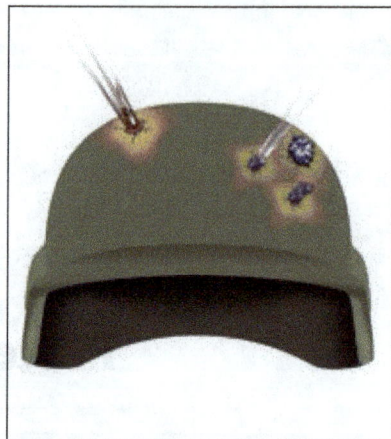

KEVLAR® is an advanced technology that helps transform the ordinary to the extraordinary. It combines high strength with light weight, and comfort with protection. Kevlar®, one of the most popular ballistic fibers, is a synthetic material developed by DuPont, with about 5 times the tensile strength of steel by weight. When a handgun bullet strikes body armor, it is caught in a "web" of very strong fibers. These fibers absorb and disperse the impact energy that is transmitted to the vest from the bullet, causing the bullet to deform or "mushroom". Additional energy is absorbed by each successive layer of material in the vest, until such time as the bullet has been stopped. In the early 1970s, DuPont commercialized aramid fiber, under the trade name Kevlar. Long aramid molecules were dissolved and then spun into fibers that were stretched as they solidified. This process oriented the long molecules along the length of the fiber, greatly increasing the finished fiber's tensile strength (Kevlar 29: 2.9 to 3.0 Gpa, weight of 1.44 g/cc). Originally developed to replace steel in the reinforcement belts of car and truck tires, aramid proved useful as well for bulletproof vests.

Personnel Protective Clothing

One of the prime requisites of protective clothing and other supporting equipments is breathable fabrics. These fabrics are widely used in many extreme cold weather and Glacier clothing. The science and technology involved to develop these fabrics is not available in the country and only few countries have successfully developed these fabrics that meet the stringent requirements of sub zero conditions. Breathable fabrics for individual protective clothing Micro porous and Monolithic based.

The quantitative requirements are as under

- Water vapour permeability 3000 to 5000 g/ m² / 24 hr.
- Water proofness min. 130 cm, hydrostatic pressure.
- Wind proofness – less than 1.5 ml/cm²/sec at 1m bar.

Chemical Protection

Protective clothing is used for chemical production is categorized from high to low, level A –D. fabrics containing electrometric barriers such as butyl rubber provide excellent protection from chemical warfare agents, but wearers can use the clothing only intermittently due to rapid on set of heat stress, motion restriction, and weight. These fabric systems are heavy bulky and subject the soldiers to heat stress under high workload and battlefield conditions

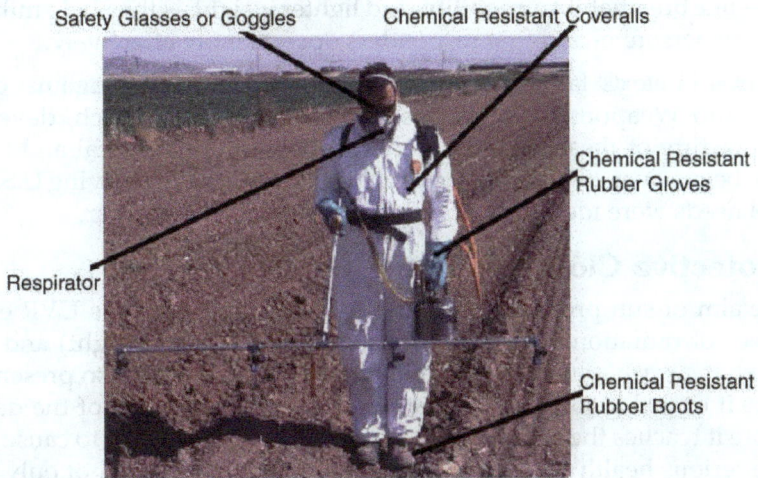

Heat Protective

Micro therm has been one of the leading high temperature thermal insulation materials. It is a better insulation even than still air and at high temperatures has a thermal conductivity as much as four times lowers than most conventional insulations such as fibre. Microtherm products cover a comprehensive range in both rigid and flexible forms, facilitating neat and effective design solutions to the many diverse thermal problems that can be encountered in military equipments.

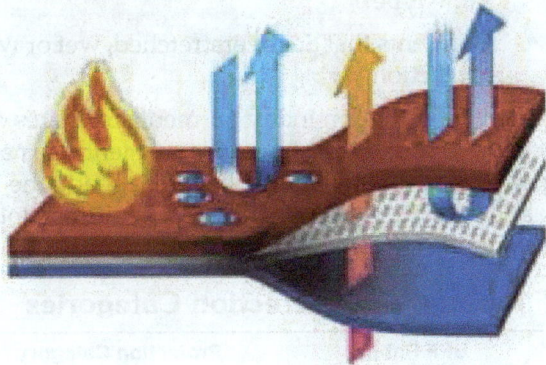

Biological Protection

Biological protection comes in two categories. The first is the protection of humans and earth from harm. It usually involves stopping disease (or other kind of damages) from either natural sources or human cause accidents. The second is protection of potential new alien life forms from harm. It involves stopping humans from damaging alien life in space.GORE™ CHEMPAK® products deliver functional effectiveness in chemical and biological environments. With a range of features and benefits — like breathability, mobility, and lighter weight — they help military and civil defense personnel and first responders operate more effectively.

Gentex's Lifetex® fabrics provide unparalleled protection against chemical, biological and Weapons of Mass Destruction (WMD). Research, development and manufacture of these superior technical textiles for chemical and biological protection began over 25 years ago and further accelerated as evolving U.S. military personnel needs were identified during the first Persian Gulf War.

Sun Protective Clothing

The aim of sun protective clothing is to reduce a person's UVR exposure. Many types of radiation emitted by the sun, mainly visible (light) and infrared (heat) reach the earth's surface. Ultraviolet radiation (UVR) is also present but we cannot see it or feel it. Ozone in the atmosphere absorbs much of the dangerous UVR before it reaches the ground but we can still receive enough to cause sunburn and more serious health problems. Exposure to UVR can cause not only sunburn but also lasting skin damage. This may result in premature skin ageing and skin cancer. UVR can also cause eye disorders such as cataracts.

UPF of a Fabric

*   Different fabrics have different UVR-absorbing properties.
*   Less UVR passes through tightly woven or knitted fabrics.
*   Darker colours usually block more UVR.
*   Heavier weight fabrics usually block more UVR than light fabrics of the same type.
*   Garments that are overstretched, wet or worn out may have reduced UVR protection

The UPF rating on many garments indicates clearly how good the fabric is at blocking UVR but the design of the garment also needs to be considered. Shirts with long sleeves and high collars, hats that shade the face and protect the back of the neck and ears are most effective. Loose fitting clothing is usually more protective than tight fitting clothing.

UPF Ratings and Protection Categories

UPF Rating	Protection Category	% UVR Blocked
15 – 24	Good	93.3 - 95.9
25 – 39	Very Good	96.0 - 97.4
40 and over	Excellent	97.5 or more

The Standard states that the highest UPF rating garments may be labelled with is 50. Garments made from fabrics with ratings higher than 50 are labelled as UPF 50+.

Sun-protective clothing offers another way to protect skin from the harmful effects of the sun. Sun-protective fabrics differ from typical summer fabrics in several ways: they typically have a tighter weave or knit and are usually darker in color. Sun-protective clothes have a label listing the garment's Ultraviolet Protection Factor (UPF) value, that is, the level of protection the garment provides from the sun's ultraviolet (UV) rays. The higher the UPF, the higher the protection from the sun's UV rays.

The UPF rating indicates how much of the sun's UV radiation is absorbed by the fabric. For example, a fabric with a UPF rating of 20 only allows 1/20th of the sun's UV radiation to pass through it. This means that this fabric will reduce your skin's UV radiation exposure by 20 times where it's protected by the fabric. Everything above UPF 50 may be labeled UPF 50+; however, these garments may not offer substantially more protection than those with a UPF of 50. Also, a garment shouldn't be labeled "sun-protective" or "UV-protective" if its UPF is less than 15. Sun-protective clothing may lose its effectiveness if it's too tight or stretched out, damp or wet, and if it has been washed or worn repeatedly.

Nbc Lightweight Overboot

It provides more than 24hr protection against chemical warfare agents. It can be fully decontaminated due to its smooth all butyl surface. Boot ensures excellent thermal isolation provided by double liner system, using a quarter inch pp-foam-polyester/viscose inner liner with a 3/8 in pp- wool / radian tex outer liner. Lighter then all existing ECW boots within its category, the boot has a polyester shell with a moisture vapour permeable (MVP) barrier layer, assuring water resistance, good breathability and dryness in all weather conditions.

Advanced EOD Bomb Suit And Helmet

2000 HELMET
Highest Ballistic Integrity in the World. Tested and Defeated Fragments Over 2000 FPS.
VISOR
705 M/S 2315 FPS
FRONT
VO (No Penetration)
1667 M/S 5471 FPS
(includes Chest/Groin Plates)
ARMS
563 M/S 1850 FPS
LEGS
563 M/S 1850 FPS

An advanced design bomb suit and helmet that offers highest ballistic protection in the world. The suit is constructed from Kevlar with an outer anti static cover of 50/50 Nomex/Kevlar and comprises of a jacket, crotch-less trousers, groin cup and rigid ballistic panels. The suit itself is light weight in comparison with other suits, with frond protection plates and this maneuverability reduces operator fatigue and increases operator effectiveness.

Ballistic and Composite Applications

Multi dimensional fabrics with yarns oriented in the thickness direction are available commercially and are built up on one insertion (single layer) at a time. A true 3D weaving process with multiple filling insertions is commercially available under the trademark 3D weaving. This process is inherently 3D from the onset and does not involve the building up of multilayer. Unlike conventional biaxial weaving that involves two orthogonal sets of yarn oriented in 0^0 and 90^0 directions, multi axial has yarn sets oriented in other directions in addition to above directions. In multi axial weaving, yarns are oriented in $(0+/-q^o)$. Triaxial and lappet weaving are examples of modifications to basic weaving.

The multi axial / multidimensional fabrics offer significant technical advantages for composite applications and eliminate some of the inherent drawbacks of biaxial woven fabrics. The fabrics offer the following advantages.

- Better load bearing capacity in different directions.
- Reduced delamination failure and higher level of damage tolerance / resistance.
- Better interface between substrate and matrix.
- Optimum realization of tensile properties due to low crimp.
- Better distribution of tension on all the yarns.
- Architecture structural fabrics can be designed that can not be achieved with conventional weaving.

The Protective textile is respective to innovative new products. There is opportunity and need for functional, cost-effective materials. But the market is fragmented and complex. Development and lead times are often long and expensive. The market is quite small but exhibits moderately strong growth and produces are generally of high unit values. Due to increasing health and safety issues at work this may be an increasingly attractive segment. Good products are needed and they must work well. It is a market that offers opportunity, but also one that demands that much development and testing be done prior to adopting new products. There may be long lead times much resistance to things new products to market. The truth is, we can not afford not to have the ideas and products.

Water Proof Fabrics

The term waterproof' is a deprecated term which implies that the water penetration resistance of a coated fabric is equivalent to its hydraulic bursting strength." It states that for a fabric to be called 'penetration resistant' then it should withstand a pressure of 10 kilopascals (kPa) when new. 10 kPa is roughly equivalent to a hydrostatic head of 1000 mm. Making a fabric rainproof is relatively easy. Making a fabric waterproof is really, really hard: you can force water through anything if you try hard enough. For our intended purposes, "waterproof" means that the fabric will withstand water pressures that it is likely to encounter during day-to-day wear. The official definition of waterproof is less simple though, and there is no universally agreed standard for it. The hydrostatic head is the height of water that can be withstood by the fabric before water penetration is observed.

Breathability

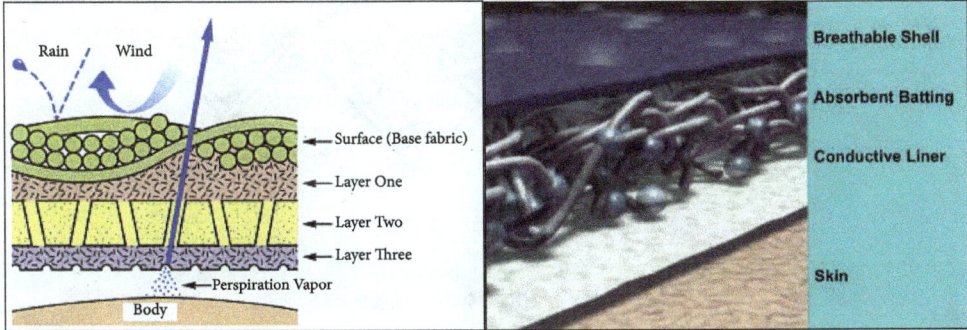

This is where the disagreements really start. There's an early stumbling block, too: the near-universal term 'breathable' implies that a material is moisture vapour permeable; it does not relate to the exchange of air, as the term might imply. Moisture vapour permeability (MVP) or moisture vapour transmission (MVT), are perhaps better terms than breathability, and mean that the fabric transports water vapour from the body. It is often-quoted that fabrics can be both waterproof and breathable because their pores are smaller than rain droplets but larger than moisture vapour. That's not really true and misses some crucial details, which will be discussed below.

Types of Waterproof Fabrics

Waterproof fabrics have been around for a long time. The Victorian Mackintosh, from which we get the word 'Mac', used rubber sandwiched between cloth to make an impermeable fabric that was waterproof but not breathable. Macs also reputedly smelt terrible and melted in hot bweather. Barbour and Helly Hansen's development of waxed jackets was important as, while still impermeable to moisture vapour, they didn't stink. Burberry developed gabardine in 1879 and it was unrivalled for 40 years. It was simply tightly woven, proofed cotton. Grenfell was the next big development, being lighter than gabardine. However, both leaked under heavy rain and were superseded by Ventile, which is still used to this day. Nowadays there are essentially four types of waterproof breathable fabric regularly used in the outdoors.

Tightly Woven Fabrics - Type 1

Ventile is the best known fabric of this type. It's been up Everest, has been to both Poles, and has been around for about seventy years. It is an Egyptian cotton woven very tightly so that its pores are very small, making it hard for water to penetrate its structure. When it gets wet the cotton swells, further reducing the size of the pores to about 3 microns (a micron is a millionth of a metre). Tightly woven fabrics are air permeable, which greatly increases their ability to transport moisture vapour. However, because water can slowly work its way through the pores, these garments can leak in prolonged wet weather and take a long time to dry. Ventile is arguably the original soft shell. Here, a mention should be made of Buffalo-type systems. Though not technically waterproof, the tightly woven outer fabric of Pertex combined with a pile liner means that water will move by capillary pressure – more on this later – to keep water away from your skin.

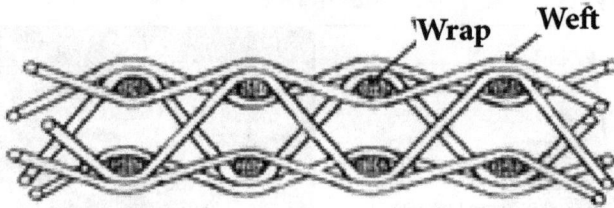

3 layer interlock woven

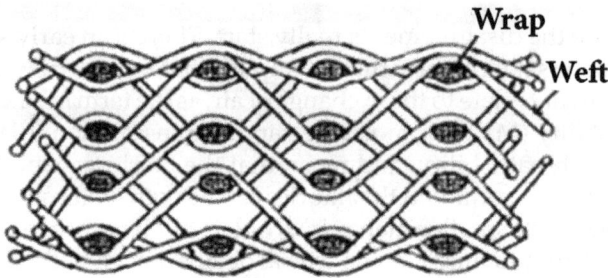

5 layer interlock woven

Fabrics with Microporous Coatings or Membranes - Type 2

PTFE (polytetrafluoroethylene) and PU (polyurethane) are the polymers most frequently used to make microporous materials for waterproof breathable fabrics. These microporous materials contain billions of holes per square centimetre that link together in complex pathways. As such, they act as a filter. They rely on surface tension to stop water penetrating them, and if the membrane or coating becomes contaminated then they can leak: water is a liquid with high surface tension, which is why it will bead on certain surfaces. Oils, such as those in sun-cream, food, or on skin, exhibit low surface tension which means that instead of beading they creep into the pores in the structure. Once inside, they affect the way water interacts with the micropores, potentially causing leaking.

Generation 1 Gore-Tex was a microporous PTFE membrane that was extremely breathable but leaked over time because it became contaminated by the wearer's oils and sweat. For this reason, Gore-Tex is now protected by a coating which reduces its ability to transmit water vapour but increases its durability. eVent is also a microporous PFTE membrane. Its structure is protected from contamination by lining the pores with a hydrophobic (water-hating) and oleophobic (oil-hating) chemical. By doing this, eVent remains air permeable, which increases its ability to transmit water vapour. Its air permeability is not high, though, and water molecules cannot be simply blown through its structure! To get through its structure is like navigating through a maze.

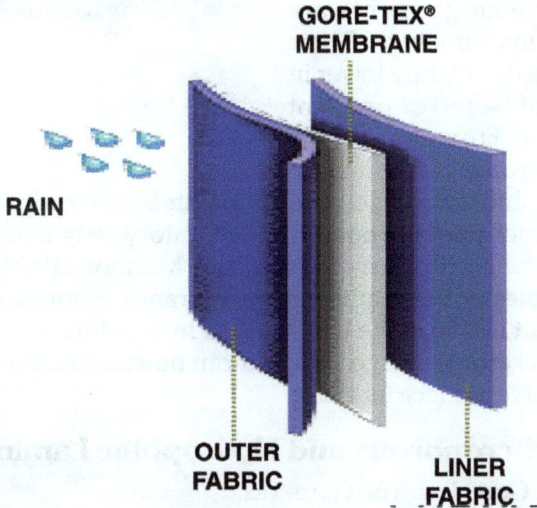

**GORE-TEX®
MEMBRANE**

RAIN

**OUTER
FABRIC**

**LINER
FABRIC**

NeoShell is made in completely different manner to eVent or Gore-Tex and from polyurethane rather than PTFE. NeoShell is electrospun, which involves dissolving a plastic in a solvent and firing the solution at a collector until a film builds up. Polartec have publicly stated that the NeoShell membrane degrades over time, though they have also stated that the hydrostatic head will never drop below 5000 mm. Relative to the other techniques used to make microporous membranes, electrospinning is still in its infancy but has enormous potential for creating excellent materials because there are so many variables, such as solution concentrations and application temperatures, that can be controlled and changed.

PTFE or PU pores are typically 0.1-10 microns in diameter. A water vapour molecule has a diameter of 0.0004 microns. Rain droplets have a diameter of at least 100 microns. Therefore, in the case of eVent and Neoshell, it is true to say that their breathability largely results from the relative sizes of water vapour, their pores, and rain droplets.

Fabrics with a Continuous Hydrophilic Coating or Membrane - Type 3

These are made from a solid hydrophilic (water-loving) film or coating with no pores. They are impermeable to air. They are usually made of a mixture of PU and PEO (polyethylene oxide). The moisture vapour transport occurs by 'molecular wicking', which can be thought of as water molecules travelling across stepping stones: the water molecules are first adsorbed to the surface of the hydrophilic material then they move to the next molecule along. This process continues throughout the thickness of the hydrophilic. Hydrophilic materials are not necessarily the same on both sides, which can help improve durability and resistance to contamination. Hydrophilic coatings stretch more easily than PTFE membranes, so stretch garments are much cheaper to manufacture. Their breathability tends to be slightly lower in lab tests than that of Gore-Tex or eVent PTFE membranes. However, their breathability is strongly affected by temperature: hydrophilics are developed to operate best at temperatures just above freezing, so sometimes perform poorly in laboratory tests that are conducted at skin temperature. The North Face's Hyvent and Marmot's Precip and MemBrain Strata are all examples of PU coatings or membranes. Sympatax (well known in mainland Europe but less so in the UK) is also a hydrophilic coating, but based on polyester. One of its key advantages is that it can be easily recycled, assuming that it is allied with a polyester face fabric.

Bicomponent Microporous and Hydrophilic Laminates - Type 4

This is modern Gore-Tex. The Gore-Tex membrane is still PTFE, but its micropores are filled with hydrophilic polyurethane. Greater durability results, and very hydrophilic polyurethane can be used that would otherwise be vulnerable to damage. There is some evidence that an air layer exists between the PTFE and PU that provides insulation, increasing the temperature differential between the inside and outside of the fabric, and this can reduce condensation. Modern Gore-Tex is impermeable to air. Active Shell, too, is impermeable to air, but its excellent breathability results from the thinness of its construction, which means that the water molecules have less distance to travel through its membrane.

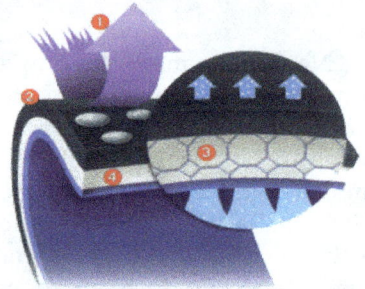

1. Wind & water completely blocked
2. Outer shell fabric
3. Water vapour molecules pushed outwards
4. Hydrophilic coating

Other Options

Some garments are regarded as weatherproof without being technically waterproof. Systems such as Nikwax Analogy, most notably used by Paramo, and Keela Dual Protection are well known for providing excellent breathability and comfort despite achieving only low hydrostatic head results. Nikwax Analogy is a two-layer fabric, the inner of which mimics the way animal fur works, relying on capillary depression. Capillary pressure is how wicking works in a baselayer, and a similar effect is seen in Analogy, so it 'pumps' water out along its fibres. The outer of the fabric is a tightly-woven cloth somewhat analogous to Ventile. Keela Dual Protection works fabric the same manner as double glazing, and much to Keela's credit, is explained very well on their website, unlike the vast majority of these technologies. Both Nikwax Analogy and Dual Protection garments tend to be warmer and heavier than conventional shell layers, so may work best in cold conditions.

Durable Water Repellence

DWR (durable water repellence) is the chemical coating applied to a fabric to increase its ability to shed water. It prevents your jacket absorbing water (wetting out), which not only makes the jacket heavy and slow to dry, but can impact on breathability. In fact, in the case of microporous PU coatings, breathability ceases altogether once wetted out. A jacket that has wetted out will conduct heat away from the wearer more quickly, potentially making them feel cold.

DWR is usually provided by a fluoro chemical or silicone coating. Fluoro chemical coatings provide greater repellence and arguably greater durability than silicones, but this is offset by their negative environmental impact. DWRs work by changing the interaction that occurs between the fabric and water. To understand this fully requires some maths. When a water droplet makes contact with a surface (eg. a waterproof fabric) there are numerous interactions that are present: between the water and the surface, between the water and the air, and between the surface and the air. There is one other crucial factor: the contact angle between the water droplet and the surface.

The DWR is not the only feature of your jacket that affects how it sheds water. As a DWR is only a very thin coating, once it has been worn out it all depends on the outer fabric the face fabric. Porous surfaces, like meshes or the face fabric of a waterproof jacket are not flat planes, and this means that water interacts with them slightly differently to if the surface were flat and uniform. A fabric with a more open weave increases the contact angle, making a jacket shed water better. However, a more open weave allows more water in to the face fabric, which means it'll dry slower. This is an unavoidable trade-off: the face fabric must be woven tightly enough to resist water penetration but loosely enough to shed rain once the DWR is worn out. The durability, tactility and many other factors are also influenced by the weave.

Some myths about DWR: 1) washing your jacket ruins DWR; 2) application of a DWR hinders breathability; 3) home application reproofing agents don't work.

- Cleaning using a specialist cleaning product or soap flakes should not negatively affect a DWR. Detergent 'masks' a DWR but does not chemically remove it.

- A DWR will only affect breathability if you apply it with a trowel. It is an incredibly thin coating and its application does not inhibit breathability.

- Home application reproofing agents rely on the original factory DWR: this is what they stick to. That means that if you wait to reproof until the factory DWR is completely removed by abrasion then you hinder the chances of ever restoring it. Heat-activation helps restore some types of treatment by orientating the molecules to provide minimal surface energy. Therefore, if the label allows, tumble drying or ironing your garment before deciding to apply a home treatment is wise: it might be that you can restore the original coating.

Geo Textiles

Geo textiles have been defined as woven or non woven fabrics having application in civil engineering, such as, interfacing of fabrics with soils to give reinforced structures or enhancing hydraulic properties of water transport.

Uses of Geo Textiles

Filtration

Filtration is one of the functions most widely performed by geo textiles. The filtration function has two concurrent objectives: to retain the particles of the filtered soil, while permitting water to pass through the plane of the geotextile from the filtered soil. These two parallel roles are the key to filtration design (Figure).

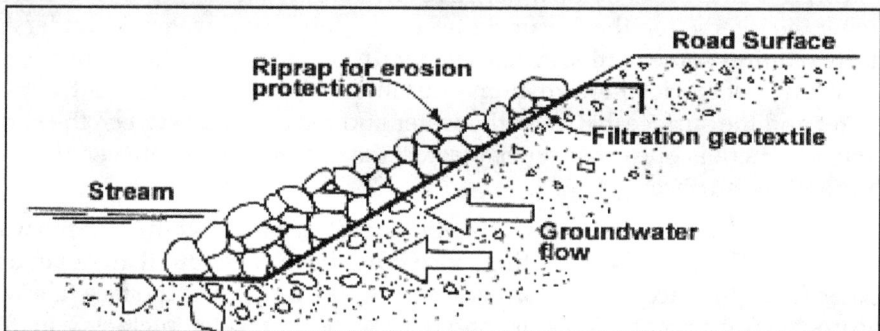

Figure: - Geotextile material used with riprap allows water movement while preventing movement of soil particles.

Geo Textile in Roads

Geo net made of polypropylene with following specifications are capable of withstanding high temperature and are suitable for Asphalt reinforcement. The Geonet are non-corrodible, inert to chemical attack, non-biodegradable and thermally stable. They are available in a width up to 10 meters and suitable roll length. The aggregate in the overlay gets interlocked in the mesh openings and a stiff layer is formed at the interface of base layer and overlay. This system prevents further propagation of cracks.

Advantages

- Control reflection cracking in overlays.
- Increases fatigue life
- Improved load distribution

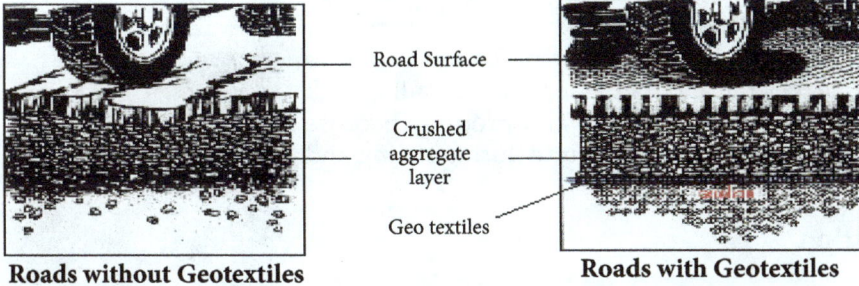

Road Surface

Crushed aggregate layer

Geo textiles

Roads without Geotextiles **Roads with Geotextiles**

Drainage

The drainage function of geo textile involves transmission of liquid in the plane of fabric without soil loss. The major difference between filtration and drainage function is the direction of flow which makes in-plane permeability critical for drainage function. Nonwoven geo textiles can assist in the collection and removal of this potentially damaging water. Geo textiles used at the native soil/aggregate interface also protect the drainage system from contamination by soil fines, while permitting the free flow of water. Composite geo textile material allows water flow within the plane of the material, rather than across it, such as behind a retaining wall.

Above: Geosynthetic base layer in construction of Landfill Site

Below: Drainage Composite

Erosion Control

Riverbanks and coastlines can be undermined and damaged by wave or tidal action. The defensive elements that require protection are:

- The in-situ soil
- The filter unit protecting the soil
- The rock armour protecting the filter

The hydraulic and filtration properties of geo textiles allow them to be used in place of some of the traditional filter layers. Consequently, a single layer of geotextile fabric can replace a succession of stone filter layers. A single bedding layer of stone is laid on the geotextile, to carry the rocks that resist the movements caused by the hydraulic forces.

Other Benefits Include

- Geotextiles have built-in, factory-controlled filter properties
- Working underwater is much easier because the filter system can be assembled above the water and lowered into position

- Less time lost through bad weather or difficult water condition

Rockfall Protection

Hill slopes composed of rocks are prone to generate rock fall and rock side hazards. Falling rock are highly dangerous to life and property because of large momentum they acquire during rolling and bouncing motion.

Solution

Use a high strength net very close to the surface profile with anchor behind the crest of the cutting and at the toe rock face. The vertical section will also have anchoring as far as possible with split bolts of capacity 3000 kg. Split bolts of 600 kg. Capacity will also be used as required by rock profile to stitch the net and to ensure that contour profile is followed to the best extent possible. The net is thus under reasonable tension and exerts a compression or inward force holding the loose mass together and prevents from easily getting disturbed due to surface movement of water, movement of fines and any untoward disturbance caused by vibrations.

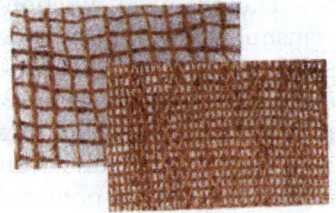

Coastal Protection-Gabions

Generally angular stones are preferred for dissipation of current and wave energy in hydraulic applications. However, based on wave surge and water depth, the stone sizes may become too large for convenient handling

Solution

Use of Gabions holding the small boulders together offer the ideal solution of coastal protection. Gabions are sausages made of polypropylene twisted ropes are appropriately woven by a special process to fabricate in various sizes. Gabions are generally available in prefabricated collapsible form with a bottom and four sides held together by appropriate binding and with a flip open top lid. The border rope is of 10mm/12mm size and body rope is of 10mm/8mm/6mm. The sizes are selected depending on the severity of the problem and the method of installations to be adopted.

Advantages of Polymer Gabions

- Resistance to acidic and alkaline environments. Immune to rot, mildew, marine organisms.
- Flexible and can easily take the riverbed contour.
- No rusting and no damage to fishes.
- No effect of water, non-biodegradable.
- High tensile strength, High abrasion resistance, High thermal stability.
- Resistance to U.V. degradation.
- Can be lifted with cranes. Suitable for underwater construction.

Apart from this there are various other applications in railways, airport runways, reservoirs and also for taking blasting impacts.

4

Medical Textiles

The term "Medical Textiles" literally means textiles used for medical purposes. Textiles apart from being a vital part of human life are long since been used in medical field, though the term has been coined very recently. Textile materials have a range of properties such as flexibility, elasticity, strength, etc. Based on these properties research work has been going on rapidly around the world towards the application of the textiles in medical field. Specialists from physicians to textile chemists and textile engineers are ready to devote themselves unitedly to apply these broad ranges of properties of textile material in medical technology. Nowadays in medicals also textiles is used in many ways. It is divided as follows;

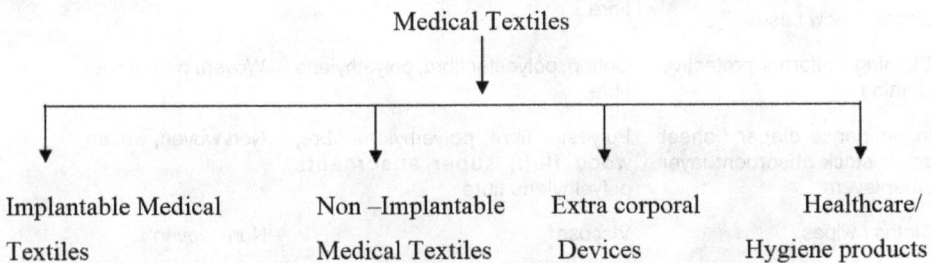

Medical Textiles

| Implantable Medical Textiles | Non –Implantable Medical Textiles | Extra corporal Devices | Healthcare/ Hygiene products |

Implantable Medical Textiles

The materials are used in effecting repair to the body whether it is wound closure (sutures) or replacements Surgery like vascular grafts, artificial ligaments, etc). There are many shapes and sizes, for duplications as found in human body. Filament, textures yarns used nowadays, which are coated to prevent leakage of blood while tissue, is forming on the inner walls.

- Carbon fibre is a popular material for tissue repair.

- Suspensors and reinforcing surgical meshes are used in plastic surgery for repairing defects of the abdominal wall. Surgical treatments of hermia in Urology etc…

- Hydrophobic snivels felt dressings are high porosity textiles made from man- made fibres designed for treatment of bums and different dermatological defects.

Non–implantable materials

These materials are used for external applications on the body and may or may not contact with skin. They are made form co-polymer of two amino acids. They are employed as covering, absorbent, protective and supports for injured or diseased part. They are different types.

Extra corporal devices

Extra corporal devices are mechanical organs that are used for blood purification and include the artificial kidney, the artificial liver and the mechanical lung.

Health Care/ Hygiene Products

Production Application	Fiber type	Yean of Fabric type
Surgical clothing Gowns caps masks	Cotton, polyester fibre, Polypropylene fibre, viscose, Polyester film, glass fibre	Non – woven, woven
Surgical covers Drapes cloths	Polyester fibre, polyethylene fibre	Non woven, woven
Bedding blankets Sheets pillow cases	Cotton, Polyester fibre, polyethylene fibre	Woven knitted
Clothing uniforms protective clothing	Cotton, polyester fibre, polyethylene fibre	Woven, non- woven
Incontinence diaper / sheet cover stock absorbent layer other layers	Polyester fibre, polyethylene fibre, wood fluff, super absorbents polyethylene fibre	Non woven, woven
Cloths / wipes	Viscose	Non- woven
Surgical hosiery	Polyamide fibre, polyester fibre , cotton, electrometric fibre yarns	Knitted

Generally the following bonding process is used for nonwoven made of pulp fibres. Thermal bonding, binder bonding, combined bonding, spun lace bonding.

Requirements opf Medical Textiles

- Non-toxic
- Non-allergic

- Non-carcinogenic
- Antistatic in nature
- Optimum fatigue endurance
- Biocompatibility
- Flame proof
- Dyes must be fast and non-irritant (if applicable)

Fibres in Medical Field

- Natural fibres like cotton, wool and silk
- Synthetic fibres like polyester, polyamide, polytetrafluroethylene, glass, carbon, polygalactin, polyglycolidelactide polymer, etc.

Major Applications

- Surgical dressing
- Spare parts for human body
- Sutures in surgery

Surgical Dressing

They are usually used as coverings, absorbents, protective or supports for the injured part. The different types of surgical dressings are:

- Primary wound dressing
- Bandages
- Adhesive tapes

Requirements of Surgical Dressings are

- They should protect the wound from environment and from infection
- They should effectively absorb exudation of wounds
- They should give mechanical support for the damage and surrounding tissue.
- They should be durable, sterilisable and also easy to handle.

Primary Wound Dressings

Placed next to the wound surface. Nonwoven with a binder content of 60% and made from cellulose fabrics are being used.

Absorbent

Similar to wound pads used in surgery, manufactured from well-bleached, carded and cleaned cotton fabrics.

Bandages

These are narrow cotton or linen, plain weave cloth of low texture, either woven or knitted. Ex: Plaster of Paris Bandage, orthopedics bandage, crepe Bandage.

Protective Eye Pad

Scientifically shaped 2 ¾" x2 ¾ x to lit over the eye used in outpatient clinic and industrial medical department.

Adhesive tapes

It is narrow, plain weave fabric having a coating of adhesive paste. It is used with other pads to conform them to the injury.

Products Used for Medical Surgical Dressings

The modern wound dressing is usually made of three layers-

(a) **Wound contact layer**: - It should not stick to the wound or cause maceration of the skin if the dressing is not changed. It can be woven, knitted or non-woven made from silk, viscose, polyamide or polyethylene.

(b) **Middle absorbing layer**: - If has to absorb blood or liquids while providing a cushioning effect to protect the wound. It is generally a non-woven composed of cotton or viscose.

(c) **Base Material:** It provides a means by which the dressing is applied to the wound. The material is coated with acrylic adhesive to hold the dressing in place, eliminates the need for bandage.

Wound Dressing

A three-layered, biodegradable wound dressing, which improves the healing process of third, and fourth degree of third, and fourth degree burns has been developed. The new dressing incorporates layers of chitosan and synthetic polymer compounds under a gauze layer, and is lightweight, flexible, odor free and impermeable to microorganisms; but permeable to water vapour and wound exudates. The inner layer of the composite dressing biodegrade becoming part of the healed skin, allowing re-application that does not disturb the wound.

Alginate for Wound Dressing

Alginate is a natural polysaccharide composed of linked linear copolymer of β-D-mannuronate and α-L- galacturonate, extracted from brown seaweed. In recent years, alginate fibres have been widely used in production of high-tech wound dressings such as hydrocolloids and hydrogels. Alginate fibres, like calcium salts, would interact with the wound extrudates to form a moist gel as a result of the ion exchange between the calcium ions in the extrudates. The alginate fibres are highly absorbent and because of their high gel forming characteristics, they can easily be removed from the wound without damaging the delicate tissues of the newly healed wound surface.

Antimicrobial Wound Dressing

Kerlix AMD is a pure cotton-treated with Anecia's plyhexamethylene biguandine agent. This antimicrobial agent resists bacterial growth within the dressing as well as reducing bacterial penetration through the product. Kerlix AMD has been approved by the US food & Drug administration and is currently being marketed by doctors and hospitals in USA. It is preferably made of a mixture of hydrophobic and antimicrobial fibres.

Requirements for Antimicrobial Effect

Textile materials in particular, the garments are more susceptible to wear and tear. It is important to take into account the impact of stress strain, thermal and mechanical effects on the finished substrates. The following requirements need to be satisfied to obtain maximum benefits out of the finish:

1. Durability to washing, dry cleaning and hot pressing
2. Selective activity to undesirable microorganisms
3. Should not produce harmful effects to the manufacturer, user and the environment
4. Should comply with the statutory requirements of regulating agencies
5. Compatibility with the chemical processes
6. Easy method of application
7. No deterioration of fabric quality
8. Resistant to body fluids & disinfections/sterilization.

Antimicrobial Products

Products with antimicrobial finish are divided into different categories. One is for purely antimicrobial purpose, to control the growth of microbes and the other is to differentiate products from other ones putting emphasis on cleanliness. Mainly the former is designed for hospital and latter is for textile and household goods. The antibacterial fibre is produced by entrapping the metal ion within a cation exchange fibre having a sulphonic or carboxyl group through an ion exchange reaction. The antibacterial metal is silver or silver in combination with either copper or zinc. The great advantage of these metals is that those are not to react with tissue.

Flexible products, such as sponges and textile wipes, which have protracted antimicrobial effect, have been developed. The wipes are impregnated wit biocides by spraying, dipping or soaking, for use in medical and other environments. The woven, knitted or non-woven product can be made from materials including synthetic fibers as well as natural and regenerated cellulosic fiber.

Bandages

Bandages are designed to perform a whole variety of specific functions depending upon the final medical requirement. They can be woven, knitted, non – woven or composite in structure. They can be classified into various classes depending upon the function they serve as.

(a) **Simple bandages** - It is an open weave cotton or viscose fabric cut into strips which have been scoured, bleached and sterilized. The problems of fraying in the plain woven bandage are overcome by use of non-fraying cotton leno bandage. The structure of bandage is more stable with crossing warp threads in the leno woven structures. These can be further coated with paraffin to prevent sticking of the bandage to the wound. Further some ointment dressing can also be given along with paraffin to aid faster healing of the wound. Elasticated yarns are incorporated into bandages to form elastic bandage for providing support and comfort.

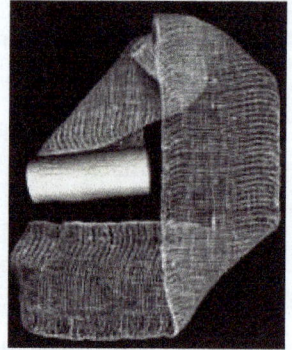

(b) **Light support bandages** – Woven light support bandages are used for sprains or strains. Elastic crepe bandages are used for sprained wrist or ankle support. The elasticized properties of these bandages are obtained by weaving cotton crepe yarns that have twist content. Stretch and recovery properties of these bandages apply sufficient tension to support the sprained limb.

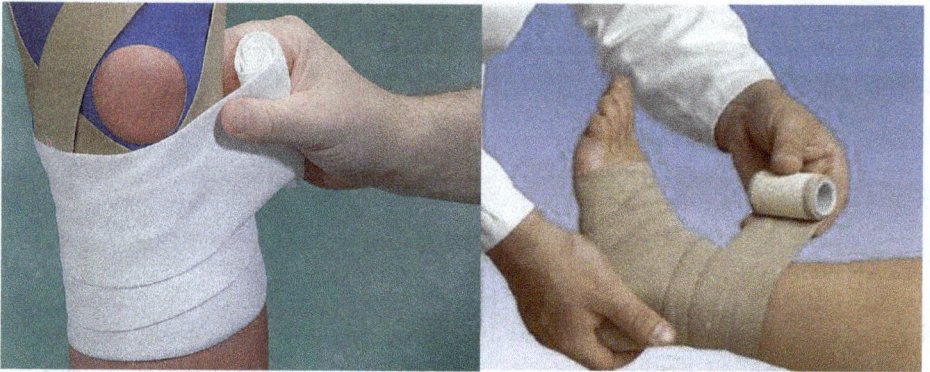

(c) **Compression bandages** – Compression bandages are used to exert a certain compression for the treatment and prevention of deep vein thrombosis, leg ulceration and varicose veins. Depending upon the compression they provide, compression bandages are classified as light, moderate, high and extra – high compression bandages. They can be woven Warp or weft knitted from cotton and electrometric yarns.

(d) **Orthopedic bandages** – These bandages are used under plaster casts and compression bandages to provide padding and prevent discomfort. Non – woven orthopaedic cushion bandages are made from polyester or polypropylene and blends of natural and synthetic fibres. Polyurethane foam can also be used. Light needle punching gives bulk and left to the structure for greater cushioning effect.

Plaster

Plasters are made up of three layers – 1) Plaster fabrics, 2) adhesive and 3) – wound pad. A simple plaster cast consists of gauze impregnated with plaster of Paris. The modern plaster fabric is made from spun bonded nonwovens of cotton, viscose,

polyester or glass fibre. The adhesive used for plaster fabric is acrylic that doesn't stick to the skin. The cushioning wound pad is made from knitted viscose fabric impregnated with an antiseptic. The highly absorbent wound pad helps in rapid absorption of secretion from the wound.

Spare Parts for Human Body

Medical sciences have developed materials for artificial grafting, for eg, heart, kidney, skin, etc. the different types of grafts are:

- Teflon woven graft
- Dacron woven graft
- Polyester knitting graft
- Polyester woven graft
- Dacron knitting graft

Sutures in Surgery

Fibres are also used as sutures in surgery. Sutures are sterile filaments, which are used to hold tissues together until they heal adequately or join tissues with implanted prosthetic devices. They are two types:

- Absorbable sutures
- Non-absorbable sutures

The health care products comprise protective clothing such drapes bed covers, towels, etc. almost 85% of all healthcare textiles are used for nursing and only 15% in the operating theatre or intensive care. By means of surveys in different hospitals wards the technical and functional requirements for healthcare, washing and reuse as well as the working conditions of the staff are reusable; these products require washability, disinfection and sterilization.

Super Absorbents in Medical Textiles

Surgical Cottons

Absorbent cotton in fibre and fabric form in used in a number of ways form is used in a number of ways in medical field. Surgical cotton is a common first aid article in very household. Also, they are used in fibre form or is converted to woven and nonwovens forms for their use as gauzes, tissues, pads and bandages on burns, wounds, etc. it is also used in the operation theaters and delivery rooms to absorb the blood and body fluids during the surgery.

Diapers – Edward Mc Lean has explored the use of absorbable cotton in diapers. The too prolonged approach comprises technology with cotton linters yielding a cleaner absorbent core for disposable diapers. Air-laid technology is facilitating the production of these diapers. Spunlace processing is an important nonwovens area with end products including disposable wipes, medical sponges and cosmetic pads. About 75% of consumers are preferring cotton-based disposable diapers and 15% of consumers are using reusable diapers, which are available in square terry cloth.

Absorbable Polymers

Polypropylene and polyethylene fabrics can be used where diapers and sanitary napkins touch the skin. In diapers, the absorbent layer is coated with super absorbent polymers. Synthetic absorbable medical devices made totally or in part from a random polymer comprising glycolide, lactide, trimethylene carbonate and caprolactone can be fabricated into a monofilament which exhibits physical characteristics equivalent to or superior than gut sutures.

Top Sheet in Hygienic Absorbents

A France based scientist has developed a nonwovens designed to be used as a top sheet in hygienic absorbent articles. The nonwoven comprises two or more superimposed layer of natural or manmade fibres, which are joined together such that the fibres of the successive layers have a denier which decreases progressively from one layer to next. This creates a fibrous structure in which the diameter of the pores decreases from the inner surface layer to the outer base layer. A Japan based company has developed a liquid permeable top sheet used in disposable garments such as diapers or sanitary napkins. The top sheet is made from an embossed nonwoven fabric, preferably comprising 60-100% by weight of thermoplastic synthetic resin fibre. Several ribs extending parallel to one another across the napkin, allows the napkin to fit evenly and comfortably around the body of the wearer.

Super Absorbable Wound Dressing

In the manufacture of a wound dressing with the ability to absorb large amounts of wound fluids and water, a superabsorbent fibre is used, preferably consisting of polyacrylonitrile. The absorptive power of this fibre is obtained by saponification of surface molecules of the fibre. Through this, the core of this fibre will remain immovable and the stability of the fibre is ensured. Another wound dressing comprises of an absorbent layer including one or more absorbent and/or Superabsorbable materials, a porous, non-sticky layer or film larger in size than said absorbent layer, a protective cover layer and a cohesive layer of an adhesive material.

A super absorbent bactericidal wound dressing called Textus Multi. It is a soft, sterile, hydrophilic dressing made from a spunbound fibre mixture. The wound contract side is coated with a porous polyethylene film that is active during all stages of moist wound healing. The product's main advantage is it provides moist environment for wound healing.

Hydrophilic Fibre & "Breath Taking" Textiles

The durable hydrophilic fibre used in the medical and hygienic sections can be obtained by applying 0.2-1.5% of a fibre treating agent to a thermoplastic fibre. The fibre-treating agent contains at least 40% of a mixture comprising 20-80% of betaine ampho-ionic surface active agent & 20-80% of dicarboxylic acid ester composition from polyalkylene adduct of hydroxyl-fatty acid ester. Dupont has developed a moisture vapour permeable, liquid impermeable sheet structure. The material could be used in surgical drapes, sterile wraps and personal care absorbent materials such as diapers and sanitary napkins. The composite sheet is durable, string flexible, highly permeable to moisture vapour and acts as a barrier to liquids, bacteria and viruses in addition to odours.

Support Hose

A post-injury support hose for patients who have sustained an injury to an extremity has also been developed. The hose is said to improve the circulation of an injured limb by applying graduated compression throughout the length of the leg or arm while providing with an opening over the injured area for accessing the patient's wound and dressing. The hose can be made in a circular knitting machine

'Acticoat' Dressing

Canadian company, Westaim biomedical, claims its Acticoat dressing provides broader and faster protection against fungal infections than conventional antimicrobial products. The dressings are layered with monocrystalline silver, known to have antimicrobial and antifungal properties, creating a protective barrier as the silver ions are consumed. A study was carried out to compare the dressings with conventional burn wound treatments. Results showed that Acticoat had the faster kill rate and was effective against more fungal species. The products can be applied to a variety of wounds including graft and donor sites and surgical wounds.

Socks

Antimicrobial socks developed by super sack manufacturing are also applicable for making shoe linings, socks and sock liners, designed to inhibit the growth of bacteria, fungus and other odour causing microbes. A thermoplastic resin is blended with polypropylene or polyethylene resin incorporating a microbial inhibitor to form an antimicrobial feedstock, which is then extruded into films, tapes or filaments used for antimicrobial products.

Artificial Kidney

- Tiny instrument, about the size of a two – cell flashlight.
- Made with hollow hair sized cellulose fibres or hollow polyester fibre slightly latest than capillary vessels.
- Fabric which is used to remove waste products from patient's blood.

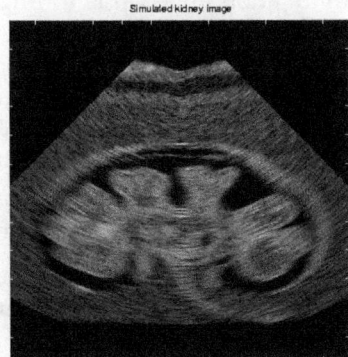

Artificial Heart

- An 8 – ounce plastic pump lined with dacom velour to reduce damage to blood and is a chambered apparatus about the size of a human heart.
- Silastic backing makes the fabric imperious to emerging gas that is not desirable in the blood.

Artificial Liver

- Made with hollow viscose to separate and dispose patient's plasma and supply fresh plasma.

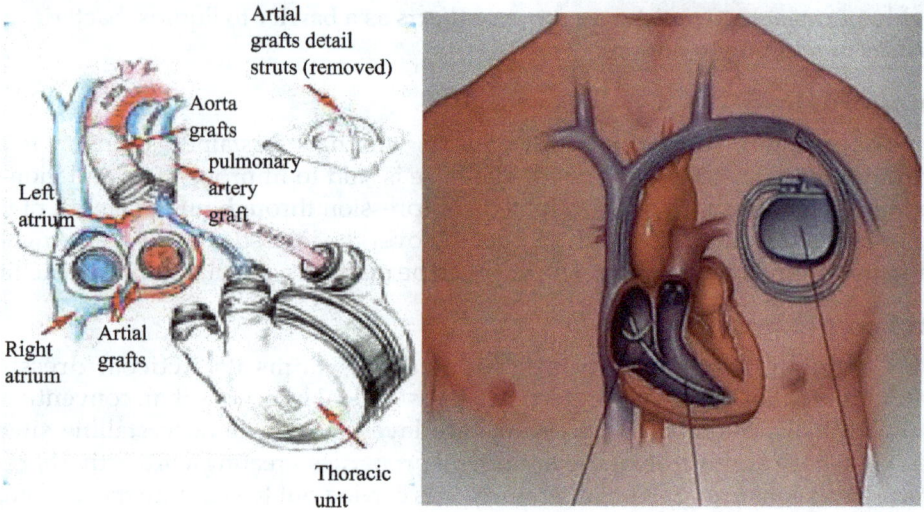

Mechanical Lung

- Made with hollow polypropylene fibre or a hollow silicone membrane.
- Used to remove carbon-di-oxide from patient's blood and supply fresh oxygen. Health care textiles

Intelligent Polymers to Assist the Hearing-Impaired

The University of Wollongong's Intelligent Polymer Research Institute's (IPRI) & Co-operative Research Center's (CRC) for Cochlear Implant and Hearing Aid Innovation, mission is to improve communication for the millions of adults and children with hearing loss in Australia and worldwide. The CRC brings innovative interdisciplinary research leading to new hearing technology devices and clinical procedures, which are nothing but the specially developed intelligent polymers, which will have a direct benefit in, improved devices for people with hearing impairment. The use of intelligent polymers raises the potential for enhanced interfacing of cochlear implants with a hearing-impaired person's own neural system, greatly increasing communication benefits.

With advent of new technologies, the growing needs of the consumer in the wake of health and hygiene can be fulfilled without compromising the issues related to safety, human health and environment. The consumers are now increasingly aware of the hygienic life style and there is a necessity and expectation for a wide range of textile products finished with required properties. This kind of value adding for textile is the need of the hour. Intelligent polymers are thus going to be a promising field for the future. Already, western countries are adopting these strategies. There is no doubt that with present facilities and technologies India can also excel in the field of intelligent polymers and their derivatives by knowing the intricacies in its manufacture and applications.

5

Smart Textiles

Smart Textiles are defined as textiles that can sense and react to environmental conditions or stimuli, from mechanical, thermal, magnetic, chemical, electrical, or other sources. They are able to sense and respond to external conditions (stimuli) in a predetermined way. Textile products which can act in a different manner than an average fabric and are mostly able to perform a special function certainly count as smart textiles.

Components in Smart Textiles

Three components may be present in smart textiles (materials)

- Sensors
- Actuators
- Controlling units

The sensors provide a nerve system to detect signals. Some of the materials act only as sensors and some as both sensors and actuators. Actuators act upon the signals and work in coordination with the controlling unit to produce an appropriate output.

Classification of Smart Textiles

Smart textiles are classified into three categories depending on functional activity, as follows:

- Passive smart textiles
- Active smart textiles
- Very or ultra smart textiles

Passive smart textiles:- The first generation of smart textiles, which can provide additional features in passive mode that is not concerning with alteration in environment are called passive smart textiles. Optical fiber embedded fabrics and conductive fabrics are good examples of passive smart textiles. UV protective clothing, multilayer composite yarn and textiles, plasma treated clothing, ceramic coated textiles, conductive fibers, fabrics with optical sensors, are some examples of passive smart textiles.

Active smart textiles: The second generation of smart textiles have both actuators and sensors and tune functionality to specific agents or environments, are called active smart textiles. These are shape memory, chameleonic, water resistant and vapor permeable (hydrophilic/ non porous), heat storage, thermo regulated, vapor absorbing, heat evolving fabric and electrically heated suits.Phase change materials and shape memory materials, heat sensitive dyes etc. in textiles form active smart textiles.

Ultra smart textiles: Very smart textiles are the third generation of smart textiles, which can sense, react, and adapt themselves to environmental conditions or stimuli. They are the highest levels of smart textiles. These may deal actively with life threatening situations (battlefield or during accidents) or to keep high levels of comfort even during extreme environmental changes. These very smart textiles essentially comprise of a unit, which works like the brain; with cognition, reasoning and activating capacities. Ultra smart textiles are an attempt to make electronic devices a genuine part of our daily life by embedding entire systems into clothing and accessories. Though the entire potential has not been completely realized, the developments so far can be termed as only rudiments of very smart textiles.

For example, spacesuits, musical jackets, I-wear, data wear, sports jacket, intelligent bra, smart clothes, wearable computer etc.

Passive smart textiles are lifeless but very smart textiles are the most dynamic levels of artificial intelligence in textiles[5]. In fact, passive textiles may not be termed as really smart since they do not think for themselves. Nevertheless they perform special functions in the passive mode and hence the term passive smart textiles.

General Methods of Incorporating Smartness into Textiles

Textile to behave smartly it must have a sensor, an actuator (for active smart textiles) and a controlling unit (for very smart textiles). These components may be fiber optics, phase change materials, shape memory materials, thermo chromic dyes, miniaturized electronic items etc. These components form an integrated part of the textile structure and can be incorporated into the substrate at any of the following levels.

- Fiber spinning level
- Yarn/fabric formation level
- Finishing level

The active (smart) material can be incorporated into the spinning dope or polymer chips prior to spinning e.g. lyocell fiber can be modified by admixtures of electrically conductive components during production to make an electrically conductive cellulosic fiber. Sensors and activators can also be embedded into the textile structure during fabric formation e.g. during weaving. Many active finishes have been developed which are imparted to the fabric during finishing.

The electronic control units can be synchronized with each other during finishing. Techniques such as microencapsulation are generally preferred for incorporation of smartness imparting material in the textile substrate. However the correct material and the correct method must be selected; based on a variety of considerations.

Applications of Smart Textiles

Smart textiles find a wide spectrum of applications ranging from daily usage to high-tech usage. Now we can review various important applications of such textiles. We would consider textiles used for the following broad categories:

- Comfort wear & Heat protection
- Medical applications
- Military applications
- Computing textiles
- Fashion
- Aviation & Space research

It should be noted that a textile mentioned in one category can find use in other categories as well. For example, chameleonic textiles (textiles that change color) are discussed as fashion wear. But they are of profound significance in the military since uniforms made out of them can help in camouflaging to protect the soldier.

Shape Memory Materials

Shape memory materials are materials that are stable at two or more temperature states. In these different temperature states, they have the potential to be different shapes. When their transformation temperature have been reached. Shape memory polymers (SMP) are materials that have hard segments and soft segments e.g. polyurethane, polyester ether styrene- butadiene copolymer. This is because the shape– memory materials exhibit some novel performance such as sensitivity, actuation, damping and adaptive response to external stimuli such as temperature, lighting stress and field, which can be utilized in various ways in smart systems.

Shape memory alloy wire and shape memory polymer films are already finding application in clothing. UKs Defense Clothing and Textile Agency is designing garment with these materials to protect wearers against heat or cold- Cold protection in leisure wear is usually achieved by laminating a layer of insulation material, consequently, the wearer needs to select the appropriate garment for facing weather conditions. A garment having variable insulation would have greater versatility and this could be achieved by using a composite firm of shape memory polymer as inter- liner. The use of shape memory alloy in multiple layer fabric systems that change shape within a certain temperature range can be utilized to change the density between the individual layers. When temperature rises, an additional layer of insulating air is formed to enhance protection against heat.

Reversible Shape Memory

Another intelligent attribute of textiles containing cross-linked polyols is reversible shape memory, which can be activated by proper choice of polar solvent and fabric construction. This reversible shape memory helps in designing of an intelligent bandage comprised of disposable and non-disposable components, which could be wrapped around parts of the body such as fingers, arms, and legs to stop bleeding. A similar approach was used to design a fabric bandage with metal threads having shape-memory, which was activated by changes in temperature. However, electric current and/or heat would have to be applied to activate the bandage, whereas the absence or presence of body fluids described above would be more advantageous in this regard.

Other recent patents and publications on intelligent fibrous materials also appear to be primarily focused only upon shape-memory effects. Some examples include:

- The preparation of polyester fabrics with durable press properties by cross-linking polycaprolactone and acrylate monomers with high-energy radiation.

- Preparation of smart fibrous composites (carbon and glass) as sensors for preventing fatal fracture by changes in their conductivity and insulating properties.

For example Clothing that generates solar power, Fabrics that beep if you risk athletic injury and bed sheets that monitor your heartbeat and physiological health. At its simplest, intelligent polymers are plastic strands that can carry electricity, altering their conductivity in response to stretching, heating or sunlight. By weaving these into clothing, and measuring changes in the current passing through them, any number of new applications are possible. The first prototype thus far has been the "knee sleeve," a training device tested last year on Australian professional athletes to reduce knee injuries. It fits over the knee like an open-ended sock. When the fabric is stretched, indicating a harmful movement of the knee, the altered electrical charge within the sleeve's polymers triggers a detachable buzzer. That tells the athlete he's got bad habits and risks anterior cruciate ligament (ACL) damage, according to Julie Steele, a biomechanics researcher at the University of Wollongong, where the device was designed. Other potential uses could include textiles such as bed sheets that constantly monitor a user's heartbeat, outdoor clothing that change insulation and waterproofing properties in response to temperature and humidity, and clothing that converts sunlight to energy.

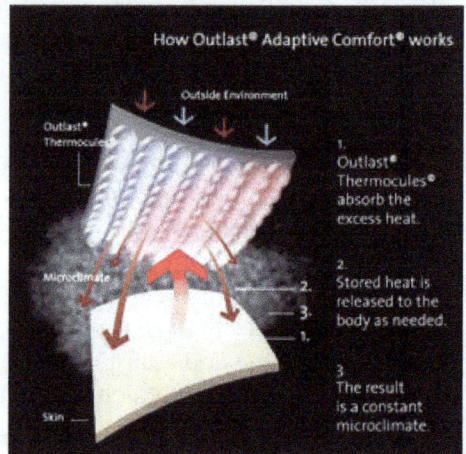

Temperature Sensitive Fabric

SWAY was multicolor fabric, basic 4 colors and combined 64 colours. SWAY can reversibly change color at temperature greater than 50C and is operable from-

40 to 80oC. The change of color with temperature of these fabrics is designed to match the application, e.g. for ski-wear 11-190C, women's clothing 13-220C temperature shades 24-320C. They developed an efficient, inexpensive method of attaching chromophores to the surface of polymers specially polyaniline. Polyprol, ploythiopene, and poly (ethylenedixoythiphene).

Heat Storage Textiles

The main object of heat storage or thermal regulatory textiles is to maintain the wearer in a state of thermo physiological comfort under the widest possible range of workloads and ambient conditions. Heat storage and thermo regulated textiles are novel comfort textiles that can absorb, redistribute and release heat by phase change in low melting point materials, according to change in surrounding temperature. National Aeronautics and space Administration (NASA) planned to put the PCMs into gloves to keep pilot's hand warm. NASA developed textiles that aimed to improve the protection of instruments and astronauts against extreme fluctuations in temperature in space on the basis of heat absorbing and temperature regulating technology. It is very difficult to produce the composite fibre by melt spinning only using PCMs as one component because melt viscosity of textile grade PCMs remains lower than required. They do not posses the required spin ability. After mixing PCMs with PEG of sufficient molecular weight, heat absorbing and temperature regulating fibre can be spun by core- sheath spinning watanabe and thermo regulated fibre containing Micro PCMs.

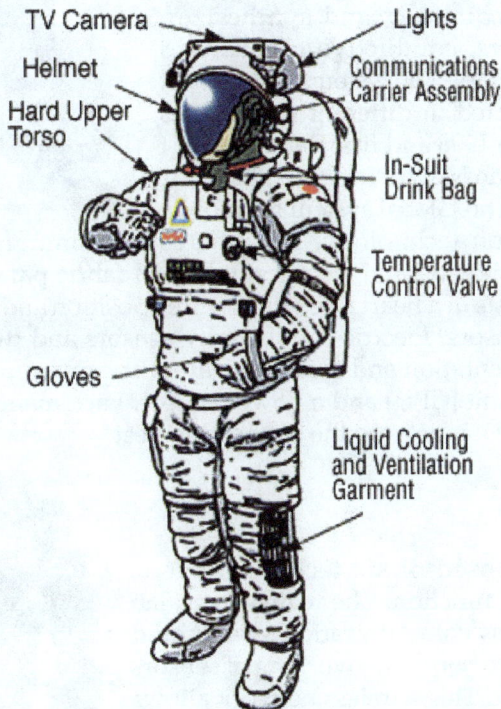

TV Camera
Helmet
Hard Upper Torso
Gloves

Lights
Communications Carrier Assembly
In-Suit Drink Bag
Temperature Control Valve
Liquid Cooling and Ventilation Garment

Ultra Smart Textiles

Very smart textiles are developing with or without the help of SOFT switch technology and related to spacesuits Musical Jackets Smart clothing (Remina Smart Suit] I –wear, Data wear, Wearable computers, Intelligent Interior surfaces, Flexible Computing Interfaces, Advanced Learning Products, Clinical Pressure Monitoring.

Spacessuits

The earliest developed Apollo spacesuits contained an inner layer of nylon fabric with network of thin walled plastic tubing which circulated cooling water around the astronaut to prevent over headings. This inner layer was comfort layer of light weight nylon with fabric ventilation ducts, than a three layer system formed the pressure garment. Net followed five layers of aluminized Mylar for heat protection mixed with four spacing layers of Dacron. These were covered with a non – flammable and abrasion – protective layer of Teflon – coated beta cloth. The outer layer was Teflon communication cloth. The backpack unit contained a life support system providing oxygen, waters and radio communications.

Musical Jackets

Musical jacket turns an ordinary jacket into a wearable musical instrument. Musical jacket allows the wearer to play notes, chords, rhythms and accompaniment using any instrument available in General musical scheme. It integrates fabric keypad, a sequencer, and synthesizer, amplifying speakers, conductive organa and batteries to power these subsystems. The smart clothing Project started in different universities of Japan and USA in 1998 and first Remina smart suit came in European Market in September 2001 commercially based on Global system for mobile GSM communication technology. The smart suit communication, functional architecture for navigation and electrically heated fabric panels for heating. The sensor system consists of a heart rate sensor, three position and movement sensors, 10 temperatures sensors. Electric conductivity sensors and two impair detecting sensor. The implementation and synchronization requires a user inter face [UI] a central processing unit [CPU] and a power source. Each main module, excluding the sensors and the UI is set into the supporting vest.

Intelligent Wear
(I – Wear)

I-clothes composed of six technical layers, each with a specific function. The team of star lab developed a wireless communication system and fabric area network to permit networking of sensors and data on clothing. This wireless network allows communication between the various layers, without

danger of radiation to the body. The network is integrated in a natural and flexible manner into the fabrics.

Data Wear

Data wear incorporates sensors at each of the body joints plotting the position on a graph, which is calculated on a computer. The sensors are made from conductive elastane. Data wear clothes consists a bunch of magnetic position sensors, the TCAS system measures the angle of each of the joints to determine absolute position of each of the limbs. It has been designed for comfort and ease. The sensors can be places to specification for individual applications. The Datawear body unit consists of jacket, trousers and gloves that are circuited or wired electronically for interaction with computer. The application of Datawear is to track position of limbs in computer data, medical imaging, measurement, ergonomics, biomechanics, robotics and animation. The whole body can be monitored by Datawear, which has a particular relevance in fields of sports injuries and biomechanics.

Smart Clothes

F A C Fashion and Design, Germany has developed smart clothes that have some excellent characteristics like rounded lines, new pocket shapes, rounded zippers, smart reflective logo, natural soft lettering , and topstitching integrated in solar cell. These smart clothes have wearable electronics as integral part of the garment, mobile, recorder and global positioning GPS systems.

Sports Jacket

A Philips Research laboratory has developed material with conductivity that changes in a predictable why as it is stretched. They made a sport jacket that can sense the arm movements of the wearer. Sport jacket could be used to monitor and assist people when playing sports.

Wearable Computer

Boeing Computer Services, Honeywell IND, Virtual Vision, Carnegie Mellon University and some other research organizations are developing a wearable computer system that is better powered computer system worn on the user's body (on a belt, backpack or vest) Wearable Computer is designed for mobile and predominately hands free operations, head mounted displays and speech input.

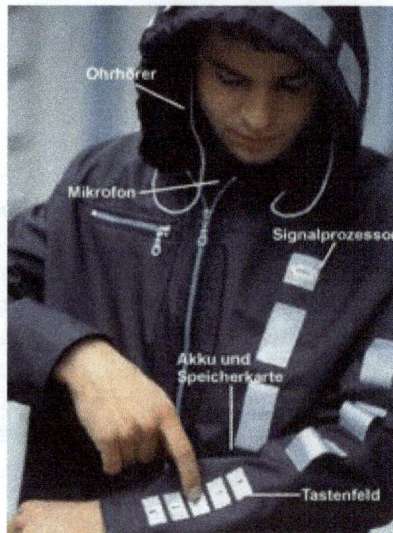

Intelligent Textiles in Medical

The fashion industry is facing new challenges: "intelligent textiles", "smart clothes","i-wear" and "fashion engineering" are only a few of the keywords which will revolutionize new and old industry within the next 5 to 10 years. The integration of high-technology into textiles, e.g. modern communication or monitoring systems or the development of new materials with new functions, has just started with timidity, but the branch already propagates an enormous boom for this sector. Especially applications for the health sector, e.g. clothes with extern monitoring systems, are already today anticipating a great demand . Developments in telecommunication, information technology and computers are the main technical tools for Telemedicine (Telecare, Telehealth, e-health) now being introduced in health care. Telemedicine - medicine at a distance - provides among the many possibilities offered the tools for doctors to more easily consult each other. For individuals, e.g. with chronic diseases, "Telemedicine" means, the possibility to stay in contact with their health care provider for medical advice or even to be alerted if something begins to go wrong with their health. This opens up new possibilities for personalized health and health care. In line with this, ongoing cutting edge research in fields such as textiles, medical sensors and mobile communication could pave the way to a better life for a large number of patients. The results of the researches will indeed make a positive impact on the quality of life for individuals in the real world.

Medical Aspects of Smart Clothes

"Intelligent Clothing" is made from fabrics that are wireless and washable that integrate computing fibers and materials into the structure of the fabrics. This technology represents a quantum leap in healthcare monitoring, producing accurate, real-time result. A garment can have some functions like a computer by using optical and conductive fibers, When incorporated into the design of clothing, the technology could quietly monitor the wearer's heart rate, respiration, temperature, and a host of vital functions, alerting the wearer or physician if there is a problem. Judging from the number of inquiries that have been received from parents, physicians and caregivers from all over the world, there is a critical need for the medical smart clothing and this need will be met in the near future.

Smart-Shirt

Georgia Institute of Technology is a university, which conducts research in the area of "intelligent fabric". Georgia Tech developed a "Wearable Motherboard" (GTWM), which was initially intended for use in combat conditions. GTWM is shown on Figure 2. Georgia Tech Wearable Motherboard GTWM is currently being manufactured for commercial use under the name "Smart Shirt" by Sensatex.

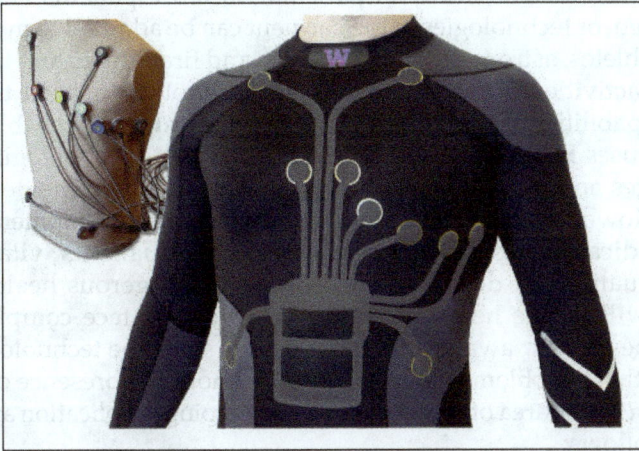

The commercial applications for the "Smart Shirt" are as follows:

- Medical Monitoring Disease Monitoring Clinical Trials Monitoring
- Obstetrics Monitoring Infant Monitor Biofeedback
- Athletics Military Uses

The Smart Shirt System incorporates advances in textile engineering, wearable computing, and wireless data transfer to permit the convenient collection, transmission, and analysis of personal health and lifestyle data. Described as "the shirt that thinks," the SmartShirt allows the comfortable measuring and/or monitoring of individual biometric data, such as heart rate, respiration rate, body temperature, caloric burn, and provides readouts via a wristwatch, PDA, or voice. Biometric information is wirelessly transmitted to a personal computer and ultimately, the Internet. The "Smart Shirt," a T-shirt wired with optical and conductive fibers, is a garment that functions like a computer. It uses electro-optical fibers embedded in the fabric to collect biomedical information. There are no discontinuities in the smart shirt. The smart shirt is one piece of fabric, without seams. Because the sensors are detachable from the smart shirt, they can be placed at any location, and is therefore adjustable for different bodies. Furthermore, the types of sensors used can be varied depending on the wearer's needs. Therefore, it can be customized for each user. For example, a firefighter could have a sensor that monitors oxygen or hazardous gas levels. Other sensors monitor respiration rate and body temperature or can collect voice data through a microphone.

The information is sent to a transmitter at the base of the shirt where it is stored on a memory chip or sent to your doctor, coach, or personal server via a wireless network like Bluetooth, RF(Radio Frequency), WLAN (Wireless Local Area Network), or cellular. It uses plastic optical fiber and various sensors and interconnects continuing monitoring human body to detect any dangerous signals or other vital symptoms. A flexible data bus brings the data from sensors to emitters and then sends to PSM (Personal Status Monitor). It is lightweight, comfortable and able to launder.

The system has shown great promise in effectively monitoring the vital signs of infants, as well as chronically ill patients, obstetric patients and the elderly. Similarly the sensor technologies in the garment can be adapted to meet the specific needs of the athletes, astronauts, police officers and firefighters and those involved in hazardous activities. Some of the wireless technology needed to support the monitoring capabilities of the "Smart Shirt" is not completely reliable. The "Smart Shirt" system uses Bluetooth and WLAN. Both of these technologies are in their formative stages and it will take some time before they become dependable and widespread. However, the "Smart Shirt" at this stage of development only detects and alerts medical professionals of irregularities in patients' vital statistics or emergency situations. It does not yet respond to dangerous health conditions. Therefore, it will not be helpful to patients if they do face complications after surgery and they are far away from medical care, since the technology cannot yet fix or address these problems independently, without the presence of a physician. Future research in this area of responsiveness is ongoing Application areas of "Smart Shirt" are as follows:

- Maintaining a Healthy Lifestyle
- Individual Athletes/Team Sports
- Continuous Home Monitoring
- Remote Patient Examination
- Infant Vital Signs Monitoring
- Sleep Studies Monitoring
- Vital Signs Monitoring for Mentally Ill Patients
- Protecting Public Safety Officers
- Battlefield Combat Care Solution

Life-Shirt

Developed by Southern California-based health information and monitoring company Vivo Metrics, the Life- Shirt, which is shown on Figure 5, uses embedded sensors and a PDA to monitor and record more than 30 physiological signs and bring standard monitoring technology out of the hospital and into the real-world environment. The information is uploaded to a computer via a datacard and sent over the Internet to VivoMetrics, where it is analyzed and then sent to the physician.

The Life-Shirt System is with 12 patents covering wearable sensor design and proprietary software algorithms. It is an enhanced, ambulatory version of an in-patient system currently used in more than 1,000 hospitals worldwide. Underlying Technology the Life-Shirt System is based on inductive plethysmography, a non-invasive respiratory monitoring technology recently cited by the FDA (US Food and Drug Administration) as the only technology capable of differentiating between different kinds of sleep apnea. It monitors breathing patterns by passing a continuous, low-voltage electrical current through externally placed sinusoidal arrays of wires that surround the rib cage and abdomen. By virtue of its design, inductive plethysmography reduces the signal interference and distortion that is often associated with other technologies, enabling clinicians to obtain a more accurate measurement of patients' respiratory functions.

Life-Shirt System Components

The Life-Shirt system consists of the Life-Shirt Garment, Life-Shirt Recorder and VivoLogic™ analysis and reporting software. The system continuously measures more than 30 parameters during daily activities. After processing the data, the system integrates subjective patient input from an on-board electronic diary, the VivoLog™ Digital Diary. Results can be viewed as full-disclosure, high-resolution waveforms or as summary reports.

Life-Shirt Garment

The Life-Shirt is a lightweight, machine washable, comfortable, easy-to-use shirt with embedded sensors. To measure respiratory function, sensors are woven into the shirt around the patient's chest and abdomen. A single channel ECG measures heart rate, and a two-axis accelerometer records patient posture and activity level. Optional peripheral devices measure blood pressure and blood oxygen saturation. Life-Shirt Recorder and VivoLog™ Digital Diary The Life-Shirt System includes an integrated PDA that continuously encrypts and stores the patient's physiologic data on a compact flash memory card. Patients may also record time-stamped symptom, mood and activity information in the recorder's diary, the VivoLog™ Digital Diary, allowing researchers and clinicians to correlate subjective patient input with objectively measured physiologic parameters .

Vivo Logic Software

Vivo Metrics proprietary PC-based software decrypts and processes recorded data using patented algorithms. It includes viewing and reporting features that enable researchers and clinicians to view the full disclosure, high-resolution waveforms, or look at trends over time. In addition, summary reports can be generated that present processed data in concise, easy-to-interpret graphical and numeric formats. Athletes could wear the garments to enhance training and also can monitor heart rate, respiration, and temperature and even listen to MP3s through the shirt. A microphone also can be embedded into the shirt. Firefighters also could wear a Life-Shirt to be monitored for smoke inhalation. On the other hand doctors could use them to monitor patients who've left their offices. While this wearable technology is developing and trying to take place in the daily market, the Indy racing league has started to use it in the field to see how a race car driver's body reacts to pressure behind the wheel.

Mamagoose Baby Pyjamas

Smart clothes technologies could help to prevent Sudden Infant Death Syndrome (SIDS) commonly known 'cot death'. The Belgian company Verhaerth Design and Development and the University of Brussels (VUB) have developed a new type of pyjamas which is shown on Figure 7 that monitor babies during the sleep. The new pyjamas are very aptly called "Mamagoose" and they draw on technology used in two specific applications: The analogue biomechanics recorder experiment and the respiratory inductive plethysmograhph suit.

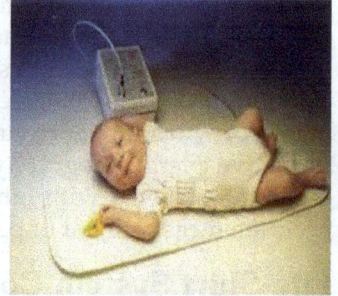

The Mamagoose pyjamas have five special sensors positioned over the chest and stomach, three to monitor the infant's heart beat and two to monitor respiration. This double sensor system guarantees a high level of measuring precision. The special sensors are actually built into the cloth and have no direct contact with the body, thus creating no discomfort for the baby. The pyjamas are made of two parts: the first, which comes into direct contact with the baby, can be machine-washed and the second, which contains the sensor system, can be washed by hand.

The pyjamas come in three sizes, are made of non-allergic material and have been especially designed to keep the sensors in place during in use. The control unit with alarm system is connected to the pyjamas and continuously monitors and processes the signals received from five sensors. It is programmed with an alarm algorithm which scans the respiration pattern to detect unexpected and possibly dangerous situations. Mamagoose prototypes have been tested on many babies in different hospitals, environments and conditions. These include babies of various weights and sizes when they are different 'moods' such as calm, nervous or upset, and when they are sleeping in different positions. To date, the results have been extremely promising.

Smart Socks

Every year, more than 50,000 Americans with diabetes must undergo foot or leg amputations. In many of these cases, poor blood circulation is the villain. It's possible to imagine having socks with built-in pressure sensors that would alert the wearer to put his/her feet up for a while. Researchers estimate that about threequarters of diabetes-related amputations might be avoided with this kind of simple warning system. Smart socks are another example of the growing push to make high-tech home medical devices a part of everyday lives. It means 'health care is coming home again'. This is one of the most rapidly growing segments of medical technology. It's driven by an aging baby boomer population, pressures to control health spending and the availability of new technology to implement decentralized care.

The Smart Bra

Scientists at the University of Wollongong in Australia are developing a 'smart bra' that will change its properties in response to breast movement, giving better support to active women when they need it most. Crafted from a new generation of intelligent fabrics, the ultimate Smart Bra will tighten and loosen its straps, or stiffen and relax its cups, to restrict breast motion, preventing breast pain and sag. Predicted to outperform any existing bra in the support stakes, it will encourage more women back to sports, and in extreme cases, stop clavicles snapping from the sudden movement of excessively heavy breasts. Fabric sensors attached to the straps and midriff of a standard bra, worn by a model in motion, will monitor breast movement and relay data in real time to a computer via a telemetry system. Information gathered from the tests will eventually be stored on a tiny microchip that will serve as the 'brain' of the ultimate Smart Bra, signaling the polymer fabric to expand and contract in response to breast movement. The Smart Bra is the first in a suite of smart textiles projects conducted by researchers from the University's internationally renowned Intelligent Polymer Research Institute (IPRI) in conjunction with the Biomechanics Research Laboratory.

Other Interesting "Smart Clothing"

There are also other "Smart Clothes" that are aimed at consumer use. For example, Philips, a British consumer electronics manufacturer, has developed new fabrics, which are blended with conductive materials that are powered by removable 9V batteries. These fabrics have been tested in wet conditions and have proven resilient and safe for wearers. One prototype that Philips has developed is a child's "bugsuit" that integrates a GPS system and a digit camera woven into the fabric with an electronic game panel on the sleeve. This allows parents to monitor the child's location and actions. Another Philips product is a life-saving ski jacket that has a built in thermometer, GPS, and proximity sensor. The thermometer monitors the skier's body temperature and heats the fabric if it detects a drastic fall in the body temperature. The GPS locates the skier, and the proximity sensor tells the skier if other skiers are nearby. Philips suggests that wearable computers will be widely used by the end of the next decade.

Next Generation Intelligence in Textiles

Intelligent textiles represent the next generation of fibres, fabrics and articles produced to respond in time. It can be described as textile materials that think and act for themselves. This means, it has keep us warm in cold environments or cool in hot environments or provide us with considerable convenience in our normal day-to-day affair. Intelligent textiles are not confined to the clothing sector alone. It is used in protection, safety, added fashion and convenience. The most important intelligent materials at present in are classified as 1) Phase change materials, 2) Shape memory materials, 3) Chromic materials 4) Conductive materials and 5) Electronics incorporated textiles.

Phase Change Materials (Pcm)

Every material absorbs heat during heating process and its temperature will rise constantly. The heat stored in the material is released into the environment through a reverse cooling process and the material temperature decreases continuously. A normal textile material absorbs about one kilo joule per kilogram of heat while its temperature rises by one degree Celsius. Phase Change Material (PCM) will absorb higher amount of heat when it melts. This thermo regulating effect of textiles can be obtained with the application of PCM.

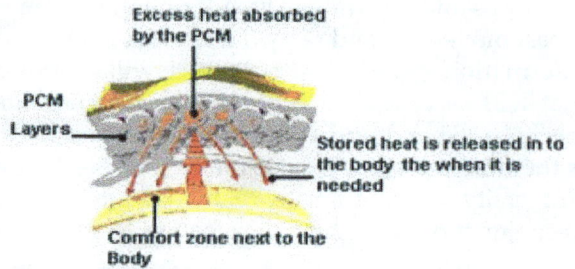

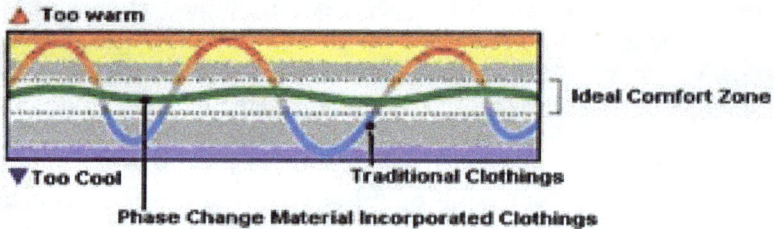

The above shown Figure describes the PCM incorporated clothing action A paraffin-PCM, absorbs approximately 200 kilojoules per kilogram of heat if it undergoes a melting process. During the complete melting process, the temperature of the PCM and its surrounding area remains constant. The paraffin's are either in solid or liquid state. In order to prevent the paraffin's dissolution in the liquid state, it is enclosed into small plastic spheres with diameters of only a few micrometers. These microscopic spheres containing PCM are called PCM microcapsules. The microencapsulated paraffin is either permanently locked in acrylic fibres and in polyurethane foams or coated onto the surface of a textile structure. Normal garments do not balance the heat generated and released in to the environment from the body. PCM incorporated textiles provide good thermal balance due to its thermo regulating effect. PCM control the heat flux through the garment layers and adjusts the heat flux to the thermal circumstances, for example, if the heat generation of the body exceeds the possible heat release through the garment layers into the environment, the PCM will absorb and store this excess heat. On the other hand, if the heat release through the garment layers exceeds the body's heat generation during lighter activities, the heat flux through the garment layers is reduced by the heat emission of the PCM. The figure2 shows the thermoregulation effect of

PCM incorporated clothing over the conventional clothing. Intensity and duration of the PCM's active thermal insulation effect depend mainly on the heat storage capacity of the PCM-microcapsules and the applied quantity. Thin high-density materials support for cooling process. Thick and less dense textile structure leads to more efficient heat release. The selected PCM is normally microencapsulated and incorporated in a textile substrate. Requirements of the textile substrate in a garment application include sufficient breath ability, high flexibility and mechanical stability. The substrate incorporated with PCM-microcapsules needs to be integrated into a suitable location of the garment design and certain design principles need to be taken into account.

Chromic Materials

Chromic materials are the general term referring to materials which radiate the color, erase the color or just change it because its induction caused by the external stimuli, as "chromic" is a suffix that means color. It can be classified depend on the Stimuli. Out of this the first four chromic materials are important and has potential to cater the market

- Photo chromic: external stimuli energy is light.
- Thermo chromic: external stimuli energy is heat.
- Iono chromic: external stimuli energy is pH value
- Electro chromic: external stimuli energy is electricity.
- Piezoro chromic: external stimuli energy is pressure
- Solvate chromic: external stimuli energy is liquid.
- Carsol chromic: external stimuli energy is electron beam.

Photo Chromic

In this kind of chromism the color change is due to the intensity of the light(UV radiation also). The photochromic dyes interact with the electromagnetic radiation in the near UV (300 400nm),Visible(400- 700nm) and near IR(700-1500nm) to produce verity of effects, which is reversible when the radiation is withdrawn. Photochromism is of Two types. Positive and Negative. In Positive Photochromism the colorless substance converted in to colored object when exposed in to the light due to Uni-molecular reaction system. Bi molecular reaction system is called Negative Photochromism i.e. from colored to colorless. The transformation is between two states that have different absorption spectra. It may be induced in one or both the direction by electromagnetic radiation. This process is a non destructive process., but side reactions may occur. Oxidation is the major cause for the degradation of the Photochromism. Main class of Photochromism is Spiropyrans. It is used in Optical switching data and Imaging system rather then the textile applications.

Thermo Chromic

Thermally induced reversible color change occur in the thermochromism. A large variety of substrates such as Organic ,Inorganic Orgonomatallic and Macro molecular systems exhibit this phenomena. Mercury Iodide salts like $Ag_2\ HgI_4$

shows color change from yellow to orange at 51°C.This is due to the reason that each compound can under go phase change at particular temperature . Majority of thermochromic systems are unacceptable simply because of the change in the color requires large amount of energy due to involvement of inter molecular transformation. Using verity of liquid crystals ,it is possible to achive significant changes in the appearance over the narrow temperature range(5-15°C) and to detect small variation in the temperature(C1°C).The thermochromic dyes used extensively in the printing of Textiles, Micro encapsulation ,coating or dope dyeing .

Iono Chromic Dye

These chromic materials are sensitive to pH. Widely used these classes dyes are Phthalides, Triarylmethans and Fluorans. In analytical chemistry these dyes are used extensively. There are no commercial application of these dyes in textiles but direct thermal printing can be used. In this process substrate contain both the color former and acid co reactant in a single layer. Simply by heating the surface of the paper with a thermal head causes the components to react and to produce color.

Electro Chromic Dye

The material that change color upon the application of Voltage are called electrochromes. This is due to oxidation and reduction process with in the electochromic material. This are of three types. First type, the coloring species remain in the solution. In the second type the reactants are in solution but the colored product is of solid. In the third type is both reactant and the color is in form of solid e.g. composite Film. Most available electochromic dyes are of inorganic oxides such as cobalt oxide, nickel oxide, molybdenum trioxide. A research is going on in MIT,USA to use thin film composite electrode material with layer by layer assembly technique, to identify whether electrochemical cell is fully charged or discharged by using color change. The most important commercial application of the electrochemic dye in the textile is of US-Military IR camouflage material (Dynam IR®) .

Solvanto Chromic Dye

The Solvantochromism is a reversible variation of the electronic spectroscopic properties (absorption and emission)of a chemical species, induced by the solvents. It is one of the oldest chromism have been described as long as ago 1878.This is used as probes for application in polymer characterization. Where they can be used to look for localized polar features at the molecular level. Chromic dyes contain highly specialized components that require extraordinary careful manufacturing technique and has great potential for both fashion and higher end market.

Conductive Materials

Exploration of human/machine interaction and wholly new types of interface sensor technology has resulted in the development of sensory fabric. These materials also afford designers new opportunities in developing for product markets. The ability to dispense with fixed casings, rigid mountings and inflexible substrates facilitates new radical possibilities in flexible, user-friendly interfacing textiles. By using conductive plastics, pressure sensitive inks and piezo films the above application succeeded in textiles. The main emphasis is currently on X-Y position sensing and pressure sensors.

X-Y Position Sensing

The structures of these materials offer the capability of reading the location, within a fabric sheet (Pad), of a point of pressure (such as a finger press). It is possible to incorporate this function into an elastic sheet structure, allowing the sheet to conform to many 3-D shapes, including compound curves, while still accurately measuring an X-Y position. The Fabric structures that provides an X-Y position function can also be used to provide accurate 'switch matrix' functionality. Interpreting electronics are used to identify the location of switch areas in any configuration to suit product requirements. Since this is done in software, an endless array of configurations can be addressed at the touch of a piece of fabric.

Pressure Sensors

Readings can be obtained from smart fabrics according to force and area. This allows the user to differentiate between separately identified inputs ranging from high-speed impact to gentle stroking. The force/area reading is versatile, as fabrics can be constructed to be more sensitive to either force or area. There are other applications for conductive materials such as heated clothes for extreme winter conditions or heated diving suits to resist very cold water. In these cases a heat or energy source is needed as the conductive material is not able to generate energy, it is only capable of conduction, to distribute the heat throughout the entire garment or suit. The advantages and benefits that conductive materials over the existing wire system are uniform temperature distribution, pliability, strength (resistance to flex and stress), non-corrosive nature, and cost effectiveness.

Other Intelligent Textiles

Stomatex®

Patterned new cold protection apparel. Cell foam materials such as neoprene and polyethylene can be used in the construction of garments. Stomatex® NE is ideal for close contour fitting apparel for unhindered body movement. Stomatex® PE is a lightweight apparel and has a significant cost advantage over neoprene. Stomatex® PE is suitable for use in multi-layered clothing systems and footwear where weight may be an important factor.

Photonic Fibres

Dielectric mirror alternative layers of two materials with different refractive indices produce Photonic band gap. It reflects light in a certain range of wavelength and absorb light out side this range this fibres can be woven in to a fabric to form shields and filters in military operations. Bar codes made with this fibre are authentic.

Hydroweave®

Patterned product is meant for comfortably in extreme cold and wet condition. Super water-absorbing polymer fibre blended into fibrous matting, this matting is positioned between a breathable exterior shell and a conductive, waterproof inner lining. The breathable outer shell can be made from a variety of woven or knitted fabrics to deliver the performance needed for a wide range of applications. The inner lining is a thermally conductive micro-porous membrane. This special material allows perspiration to escape, and keeping the wearer cool and dry. The advantages are

- Evenly distributes cooling effect over the entire fabric.
- Flexibility.
- Wearer will feel good comfort.
- Machine-washable.
- Re-usable.

Electronic Systems Incorporated in Textiles

There have been some very exciting developments recently regarding clothing with electronic systems incorporated into the constituent fibres and fabrics. Some examples of this are:

1. Music t-shirts- they allow to the wearer listen his/her favorite music stored on a chip, or to tune into the favorite radio station. They can also have moving images on the back.

2. Businessman garments-, which has a microphone, incorporated in the collar, a display, and a personal digital assistant in the sleeve.

3. Solar energy re-charges jacket- it includes some tools for creative playing and communication, such as a camera, display and microphone attachments.

4. Massage kits- It gives a soothing massage to the wearer that can be regulated depending on the level or relaxation desired by the user by applying vibration and pressure.

The smart textile market is to innovative new products. There is opportunity and need for functional, cost-effective materials. But the market is fragmented and complex. Development and lead times are often long and expensive. The market is quite small but exhibits moderately strong growth and produces are generally of high unit values. Due to increasing health and safety issues at work this may be an increasingly attractive segment. Good products are needed and they must work well. It is a market that offers opportunity, but also one that demands that much development and testing be done prior to adopting new products. There may be long lead times much resistance to things new products to market. The truth is, we can not afford not to have the ideas and products

6

Agrotextiles

With the continuous increase in population worldwide, stress on agricultural crops has increased. In order to keep grains, vegetables and flowers, it is necessary to increase the yield and quality of agro- products. However, it is not possible to meet fully with the rationally adopted ways of using pesticides and herbicides. Further, methods are expensive and have long lasting ecological impact on soil as well as delivered product. Today, agriculture, horticulture area has realised the need of tomorrow and opting for various technologies to get higher overall yield, quality and tasty agro-products. Adopting the hi-tech farming technique, where textile structures are used, could enhance quality and overall yield of agro-products. Textile structures in various forms are used in shade house/ poly house, green house and also in open fields to control environmental factors like, temperature, water and humidity. It also poly avoids agro-products damage from wind, rain and birds. Agro textiles like sunscreen, bird net windshield, mulch mat, hail protection net, harvesting net, etc can be used for achieving the above goal.

Need of Agro Textiles

- They prevent the soil from drying out increase crop yield
- They improve product quality
- Agro textiles protects farmer from harmful pesticides
- Thermal protection textiles are treated with ultraviolet ray stabilizers.
- The best-known products are shade netting and thermal screens, the use of which can save up to 40% on energy in heating greenhouses
- Their use improves the quality

Forms of Agro Textiles

There are different forms of agro textiles are available such as:

- Nets

- Sheets
- Woven
- Nonwovens
- Knitted
- Novel & Coated

A comprehensive range of woven and knitted fabrics, nets and meshes for landscaping, horticulture and agriculture, protective textiles it is mainly used.

Fibers Used

There is use of synthetics as well as natural fibers in agro textiles. Fibers used in agro textiles are as follows: -Quality of fruit prevents staining and improves uniformity of color

- Nylon
- Polyester
- Polyethylene
- Polyolefin
- Polypropylene
- Jute
- Wool

Among all these fibers the Polyolefin is extensively used where as among natural jute and wool is used it not only serve the purpose but also after some year it degrades and act as the natural fertilizer.

Properties Requirements

The properties required for agro textiles are,

- Weather resistance- It must work effectively in cold as well as hot climatic conditions
- Resistance to microorganisms-it must resistant to microorganism to protect the living being
- Stable construction- the construction must be such that it must be stable for any application
- Lightweight- the weight of the fabric should be such that it will bare by the plant.

Areas of Applications

Agriculture, horticulture, protective textiles and landscaping: applications are in woven tape ground covers, wind-break screens, frost protection covers, hail netting, insect screens, silage protection, ventilation screens, shading and reflection screens, bind netting, etc.

Types of Products

Wide varieties of agro textile products are available and the selection of suitable type of product depends on the protection that the crop-Selection of the Agro textile is greatly influenced by the geographical location. At some location agro textiles are used to protect the plantation from excessive sunlight while at some places it is expected to protect plant from cold. Therefore selection of agro textile is done as per the location and the desired protection from the external agencies. With the use of high quality agro textile quality and yield of agro products can be enhanced. Some of the agro textiles explained are

- Sunscreens
- Bird protection net
- Plant net
- Harvesting net
- Windshield
- Root ball nets
- Turf Protection Net
- Mulch mat
- Nets for covering pallets
- Packing materials for agricultural products

Soil Covers

The relevant parameters for an agro textile, used as soil cover, will be determined based on laboratory tests and field experiments. The relevant parameters for soil cover fabric features:

- Woven polypropylene fabric
- Controls weed growth for agricultural settings
- Permeable (allows water to pass through
- Colored stripes every 12" make for easy plant alignment
- Ideal for greenhouses or outdoors where weeds need to be controlled
- UV stabilized for extended life

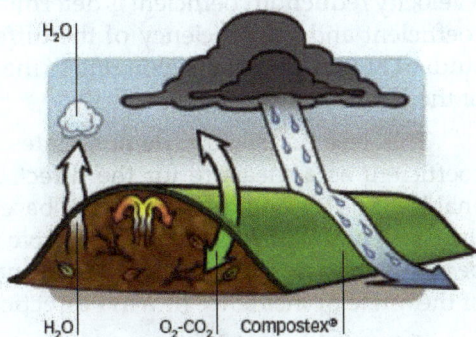

Sun Screen

In order to protect fields and greenhouses from the intense solar radiation for healthily plant growth and good harvest, sunscreen nets with open mesh construction are used to control sunshine and amount of shade required. Sunscreen fabrics are available with different shade coefficient like 35% 50% 65% 95%. These net fabrics allow the airflow freely, so the excess heat does not built up under the sunscreen.

Wind Screens

Research is performed into the various parameters characterizing agro textiles used as windscreens. The often-used 'total open area' is not an unequivocal parameter, opening size distribution and characteristic opening give more information on the structure of an agro textiles. To mutually compare the wind velocity reduction of various kinds of synthetic windscreens under all circumstances a velocity reduction coefficient is determined. The usability of the velocity reduction coefficient and the efficiency of the different kinds of synthetic windscreens are studied in a wind tunnel belonging to the International Centre for Eremology (ICE) of the University of Gent.

This research clearly demonstrates the usefulness of the velocity reduction coefficient as a measure for the direct comparison of synthetic windscreens; it enables thus the choice of a material based on the velocity reduction coefficient. In the wind tunnel, the effect of successive screens on wind breaking is studied at a perpendicular angle of incidence of the wind direction, together with the influence of the angle of incidence of wind direction with the windscreen.

The results of the measurements in the wind tunnel at scale model under stable and perfectly controllable conditions will be compared with the results of the measurements obtained under unstable conditions.

Shading Screens

In the research on the influence of shading screens used as shelter for plants, a comparison is made between temperature and relative humidity respectively beneath the shading screen and in the open air. In addition, the effect of light intensity will be studied. Screens in glasshouses: a preliminary research with a light box was started to measure the passage of visible light and photosynthetic active rays through an agro textile used as screen in glasshouses. In a later stage, with field experiments in glasshouses, the relevance of the measurement of UV-rays will be investigated. The per centage of shadow varies according to the density of the threads. They currently offer 45%, 65% and approximately 85% shadow. Shading requirements vary according to the area and crop type. Available in various colors: black, white, dark green, light green, green and white, blue and white. Black is the most common color since this guarantees most shade.

Agro Nets for Protection of Crop Against Birds

Open mesh nets are effective means of protection and can be laid over the plants easily. The advantage of using the nets over the plants is that the nets only have to be erected once in the season. These nets will not damage to the plant because of its light weight initially in the olden days there is extensively used to fire shots in order to keep the birds away from the crop but that was requiring a continuous monitoring. Knitted flat tape nets are available in a wide range of densities for shade, reduced sunlight intensity, fruit support, privacy screening and animal protection. The nets are practical, economical and easy to install; creating ideal growing conditions by avoiding overheating, scorching and moisture loss. The low shade factor nets are used for growing vegetables, while those with medium light-reduction/screening offer ideal conditions for storage areas, cultivating flowering plants/houseplants and acclimatizing plants moved out of greenhouses. Open –mesh net fabrics are used as a means of protecting fruit plantation crops and vegetables from flocks of birds. Plantation area is covered from top and side to stop the birds from getting into the fields. The advantage of using pets as a cover other means of protection is that the nets only have to be erected once in the season.

Plant Nets

These are the made from polyolefin type of fiber which is used for keeping away the fruit from the damp soil. It is mainly used for the tomato type of plant. The GSM of the nets are 30-40. Fruits, which grow close to the ground, can be kept away from the damp soil by allowing them to grow through vertical or tiered nets in order to keep the amount of decayed fruit to a minimum.

Protective Membrane

Textile works with any type of ground and offers an equal performance in agricultural, residential applications or in drainage of the roads. Use it to prevent bad grasses or sand to block the crucial drains. This permeable textile under high-pressure and is extremely easy to install. Available in rollers of 1 feet 6 inches out of 11 feet 6 inches

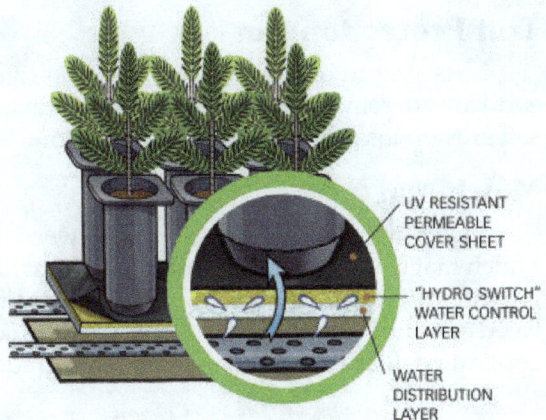

UV RESISTANT PERMEABLE COVER SHEET

"HYDRO SWITCH" WATER CONTROL LAYER

WATER DISTRIBUTION LAYER

Separation Membrane

Remarkably strong, versatile, and effective. This fabric meets the separation requirements of most landscaping projects. Use Garden Helper to control weeds around trees and borders, prevent soil contamination, control erosion, and much more.

- Available in rolls covering 107 sq. ft. to 5164 sq. ft.

Weed Control Fabric

Prevent weed growth naturally with this protective fabric based on Tex-R® technology. You'll find plenty of uses for this multipurpose membrane. And it's breathable, letting air and water through effortlessly.

- Available in rolls covering 86 sq. ft. to 1506 sq. ft. Needle punched nonwovens fabric is mainly used for the purpose of weed control applications

Green Houses

Film greenhouses for the culture of plants growing in the half-light, which eliminates the disadvantages from usual films for greenhouses for this kind of use. For the culture of mushrooms, intensive in work, we produce woven EP highly resistant, who are used for example as tablecloths of breeding on racks of production.

Harvesting Net

Harvesting nets are extremely helpful to those countries where labour charges are costlier. With the application of such nets for harvesting purpose the labour cost could be reduced considerably. They are laid on ground or tied under the tree so that fruits fall directly on to them. In Windshields are used in forming to protect fruit plantation from wind this way hard as well as soft fruits can be harvested with minimum proportion of is not damage and to prevent damage to plants. It also prevents plants being cooled by the wind. These measures create favorable climate condition for growth and improve harvest yields. Windshields can have large or small openings depending on the amount of wind protection required.

Truf Protection Net

Nets are put over the grassy areas on riverbanks. Dykes, etc so that lumps of earth are not removed while animals are grazing them. This will help in minimizing soil erosion loss and improve conservation.

Mulch Mat

Mulch mats are used to suppress weed growth in horticulture applications. Mulch mat covers the soil blocking out light and preventing the competitive weed growth around seedlings. This also reduces the need for herbicides required for weed control. Needle punched non-woven and black plastic sheet are used for this application, Biodegradable and non-biodegradable type or mulch mats are available.

Nets for Covering Pallets

For safe transportation of fruits and vegetable to the market individual boxes are collected into larger units and these boxes are covered with wide, large mesh nets on pallets to stop the boxes being turned upside down or squashing each other. This prevents damage to goods during transportation.

Root Ball Net

For safe and speed growing of young plants it is extremely important that root system is not damaged when they are dug up, transported or replanted. Normally the root balls are wrapped in cloth. Elastic netting tubes are an effective alternative to this. The soil and root system are held together by gentle pressure from the elastic yarns surrounding them, so that root balls and the earth sticking to them can be transported safely. When the plants are transported the nets on the outside do not have to be removed since the roots can protrude through the nets. Particulars advantage of tubular net wrapping is the ease of handle.

Packing Materials for Agricultural Products

Nets can be used in the form of sacks, bags and tubes for packaging of farm products for many end uses. If includes:

• Packing sacks for vegetables.

• Tubular packing nets for fruits

Net structures are preferred because of their high strength, low weight transparency, air permeability and cheapness. The pressure exerted on soft fruits is very less because of the use of flat tape yarns. Desired open-mesh structure can be produced.

Magic Carpets

Introduction

Erosion and desertification are major problems in many parts of the globe. Erosion is caused when the organic binding matter, such as the plants and organisms, in the soil are destroyed by the elements. Ground matter can be removed by water, ice or the wind and the top soil is the first layer to disappear. There are many countries, landowners and farmers who would like to be able to utilize desert lands for crop growing and other practical applications that would help to improve the livelihoods of the indigenous people. However, even if there is potential to regenerate desert land, the problem, in addition to the organization of effective irrigation systems, is that the binding root system of the plants does not grow fast enough to permit the vegetation to keep the surface soil in place or for the soil to retain its moisture.

Anti Erosion Matting

Anti erosion matting - also called the Magic Carpet - has been developed as a prototype to provide a growing medium for plants which should help counter the problems of top soil erosion. The matting is made from harvesting residue, waste wood, waste paper, plant fibre pulp and peat. Composted biowaste is also suitable to use as a raw material.

Manufacturing the Magic Carpet

The raw materials are crushed and then they are mixed together. Various kinds of pulp that assist plant growth, such as plant starch and proteins from the wood and food processing industries can be added to the mixture. In this way, the matting provides sufficient nutrients for the plants that will bind the soil. During the manufacturing process, long fibres can be added to the matting in a binding criss cross pattern or the matting can be overlaid with a large mesh fastening net or a biodegradable surface to help secure the soil. The Magic Carpet is manufactured in rolls between 50 centimeters and 2 meters wide and then it is compressed to a thin layer measuring between 5 and 10 millimeters thick. The selected seeds and seed assortments are added between the layers of the matting during the final stages of manufacturing. The seeds only begin to germinate when the matting is laid in place on the soil and watered. Using this method, it is possible to choose the kinds of plants best suited to the area where the carpet is being laid. Particular consideration should be given to plants that will bind the soil suffering from erosion most effectively.

Securing the Magic Carpet

The rolls of matting are transported to the selected site and pegged down using a machine specifically designed for the purpose. In smaller areas, the matting can be attached manually. The pegs are made from wooden stakes between 20 and 30 centimeters in length. Pegging with these stakes ensures that the matting stays in place while the seeds it contains have a chance to germinate and the root systems become strong enough to bind the matting to the soil. In some circumstances, for example, in areas with favorable weather conditions and little wind, the use of wooden stakes is not necessary.

Advantages of the Magic Carpet

- The carpet is extremely easy to manufacture and does not require complicated production equipment. The raw materials needed to manufacture the anti erosion matting are readily available worldwide.

- Waste materials from other processes can be used for manufacturing the matting rather than being discarded. These include harvesting residue, waste wood, waste paper, waste pulp, residual peat, recycled textiles, straw and grass fibre, recyclable organic waste produced by local communities and waste materials from cellulose manufacturing. The use of recyclable organic matter is encouraged.

- The matting is ecologically sound because it prevents desertification; the carpet and stakes decay in time, naturally becoming part of the soil; and the manufacturing process uses low grade materials or materials that would have otherwise been thrown away. The matting is easy to handle and to store.

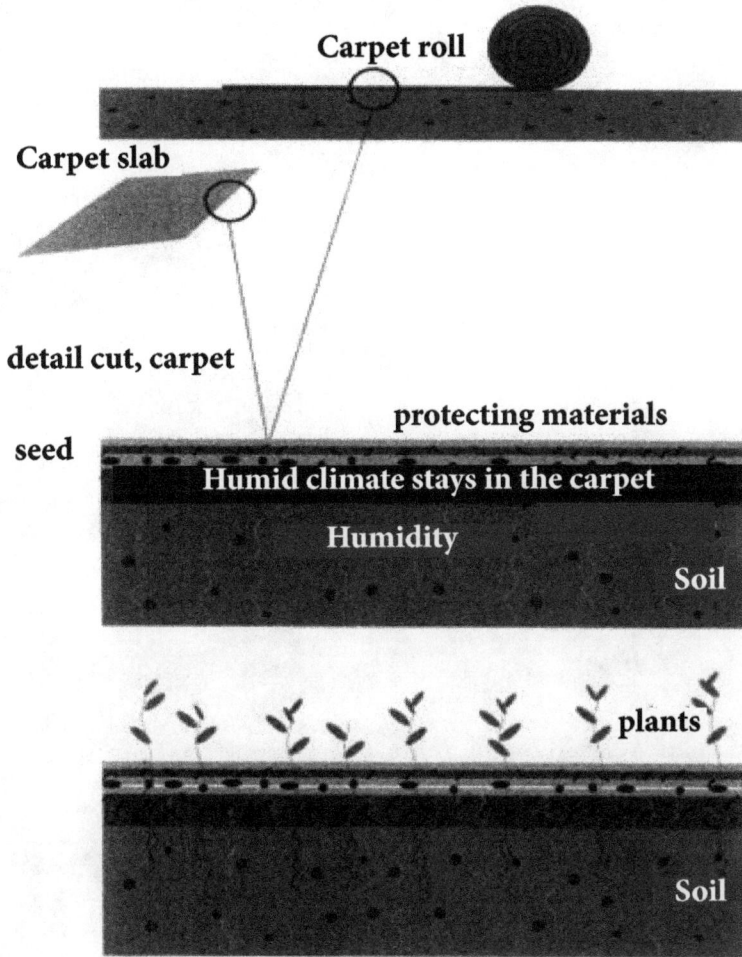

- The matting is relatively easy to transport compared with topsoil which is much heavier. The carpet is produced as either rolls or slabs which are covered with a decomposable packing paper for transportation and packing. The matting can be laid either by machine or manually.

- Once the carpet is attached to the soil, it evens out the climatic temperature extremes. It protects the soil against the hot sun during the daytime and at night; it prevents the release of heat. The carpet absorbs moisture so effectively that dew soaking into it during the night is retained because it is unable to evaporate during the course of the day.

- The carpet can be cut, for example, into narrow strips, to ensure that it is useful for all applications and that it can fit into a particular space.

- When laid down and pegged, the matting flattens the existing soil and moulds itself round the terrain it is being laid on. It binds the ground beneath it and comfortably fits over protuberances on the surface.

7

Automotive Textiles

The growth of automotive textiles is very good in lost decades. There are few driving forces behind the growth of automotive textiles. These forces could be

- Improvement in the standard of living of people resulting in the greater demand for personal vehicles.
- A car interior has become more and more important as people are spending more time in cars.
- For better fuel economy the trend is towards light weight vehicles replacing metal by fibre composites in most of the applications.
- Stringent legislations led to more safety devices in the vehicles in the form of air bags and seat belts.
- Eco logical reforms for recycling of used cars have increased the amount of textiles in an automobile.
- Apart from interiors and safety, textiles have also come up with the solution to engineering problems such as tyre reinforcement, acoustics protection, gas and air filtration.

Fibres Used

Application	Fibres used
Seat covers	Nylon, polyester, pp, wool
Seat belt	Polyester
Carpet	Nylon, PET, PP
Air bags	Nylon 66,nylon 46
Tyre cords	Viscose rayon, nylon, Kevlar
Composites	Carbon, glass, armid

Car Interiors

People are spending more time in car due to increased traffic density, greater mobility and long distance traveling. Car interiors becoming increasingly important with raised consumer expectations. Car interiors comfort is an important priority reflecting in their costs of car interiors. Today, over 90% car seat covers are made of polyester filament yarns. Apart from good abrasion resistance and UV resistance, polyester also offers good tearing strength, ease of cleaning, and mildew resistance. Wool is sometimes used due to its flame resistant characteristics but it is only limited to upper end cars. Polypropylene is also striving to capture market but it is associated with certain inherent drawbacks such as lack of dyeability, low thermal and abrasion resistance.

Seat Belts

Wearing of seat belt can reduce fatal and serious injuries by 50%. All new cars in western countries have diagonal seat belts made of 250 grams of fabrics. Seat belt is an energy absorbing device, which controls the forward movement of wearer in an event of sudden deceleration of vehicle. Seat belt is designed to keep the load imposed on victim's body during crash, down to survivable limits and deliver non recoverable extension in an event of crash. This non recoverable extension prevents the occupant from being pulled back into their seats and sustains whiplash injuries soon after the impact.

Today in modern cars seat belts are designed to hold the occupants in correct position to strike air bag then it is inflated. Thus in modern car seat belts and the air bags are not substitute to each other but complementary. Due to non recoverable stretch the seat belts has to be replaced after major accidents. Polyester is the most preferred fibre for seat belts as it satisfies the requirements of maximum extension up to 24 to 30%, good abrasion resistance, heat and light resistance and light weight. About 90% seat belts are made from polyester only. Basically, seat belts are narrow fabrics (mostly 46 mm) from polyester filaments. They can either be formed spun dyed yarns or piece dyed.

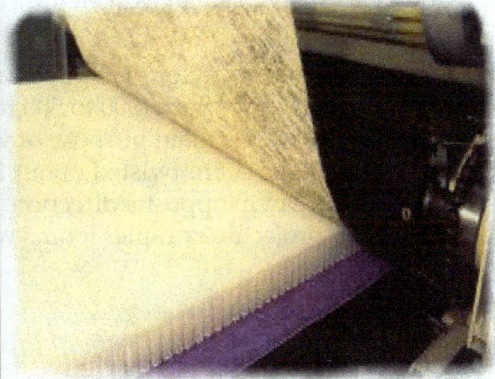

Air Bags

In most countries air bags are mandatory for all passenger cars due to stringent in legislation. In 2002 alone, air bags system has contributed up to 20% reduction in fertilities resulting from front collision. Earlier air bags were considered as substitute to seat belts and were only limited up to high speed sports cars. But today, air bags are working in coordination with seat belts. In fact, air bags cushion an occupant in an event of crash. This helps in avoiding the heat on collision.

The working of air bag is precision application. In just 0.03 seconds air bags should begin and by 0.06 seconds after crash bag should be fully inflated. Air bag may build into stearing or in some other strategic location. Mostly, nitrogen gas is used in air bags. Fabrics used for air bags must be able to withstand force of hot gases and they must not penetrate through fabric. Air bags are typically oven from HT multifilament nylon 6.6. Nowadays, one piece weaving system, produces air bag directly on loom. But earlier it was two piece seen together with suitable threads. Also research is going on to use nonwoven for this end use. Air bags can be coated or uncoated. Typically, front air bags are uncoated. Size of air bags may vary according to position.

Carpets

There is about 3.5 to 4.5 sq. mts. carpet in each car. Apart from ethical and sensual comfort, carpets also play significant role in acoustic and vibration control. Increasing popularity of multi purpose vehicles and headliner carpets had also increased the demand of the same. Road noise is considered as an environmental pollution in few countries. There are pressures on automobiles to reduce external noise about 50%. Carpets are contributing to solve this problem. Carpets by providing thermal and acoustic protection, thus directly contributing to safety.

Tyre Cord Fabrics

Tyre cord fabric is skeleton structure, which holds the uniform rubber mass of tyre. Tyre cord fabric has a tyre reinforcement performs to basis functions:

- It gives dimensional stability to tyre. Tyre is a pressure vessel and cord fabric keeps it dimensionally stable.

- Cord fabric also gives skeleton stage, fatigue and braises resistance, load carrying capacity.

Mainly polyester, nylon, HT rayon and Kevlar is used in tyre cord. Warp consists of any of above yarn (300 to 500 tex) with very few weft threads 1 to 2 PPI of 15 to 25 Decitex. The main purpose of weft thread is only to keep warp threads together. Single yarns are twisted about 300 to 500 TPM and then doubled with same twist level but in opposite direction. Weaving is mostly carried out on heavy shuttle looms; projectile or rapier looms without temples with batching motion.

8

Filtration Textiles

Textile that is primarily used for its performance or functional properties and not for its appearance or aesthetics is known as technical textile. The industrial fabrics that are used for various industrial applications are also classified as technical textiles. As such, technical textiles are the high performance fabrics that are basically used for non-consumer applications. Some textile academicians also include finished products such as ropes or tarpaulins, and parts of other products, such as tyre cord for tyres or cover stock for diapers, in the definition of technical textile. As per reveal of Prof U J Patil and Prafull P Kolte, in the coming decades, filter fabric filtration will play a very critical role in day to day life, and there is no single type of fabric being used in all the applications, for the usage of the filter fabrics varies according to their end use. Textile materials are used in the filtration of air, liquids, in food particles and in industrial production. Filtration fabrics are used widely in vacuum cleaners, power stations, petrochemical plants, sewage disposal, etc. Textile materials, particularly woven and nonwoven are suitable for filtration because of their complicated structure and thickness. Dust particles have to follow a tortuous path around textile fibres. Thus, due to their structure, they have high filtration efficiencies. A filter fabric intended to use for heavy chemical filtration may or may not be used at high temperatures.

Fibres Used for Filtrations

Generally, for filtrations, synthetic fibres are used because:

1) They have reduced fabric weight

2) They are having higher strength

3) Easier handling and replacement

4) Easier separation of filter cakes

5) Resistance to rot

6) Higher filtration rate

7) Higher fatigue resistance

8) Good dimensional stability

9) High temperature resistance

10) Better abrasion, corrosion and chemical resistance

As fibre diameter increases, filtration efficiency decreases. Also, void volume, which is required to reduce the pressure drop is more in case of nonwoven (98%) than that of woven or knitted (70%), thus nonwoven are advantageous to use.

Non-Crosslinked Coating on Substrate

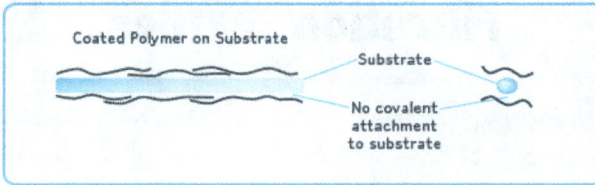

Coated Polymer on Substrate

Substrate

No covalent attachment to substrate

Crosslinked Copolymer Precipitated onto Substrate

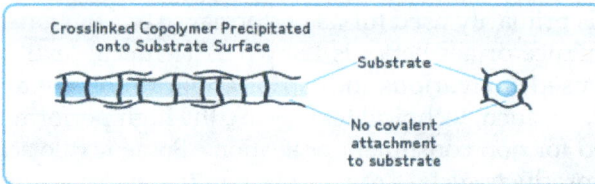

Crosslinked Copolymer Precipitated onto Substrate Surface

Substrate

No covalent attachment to substrate

Grafted to Substrate

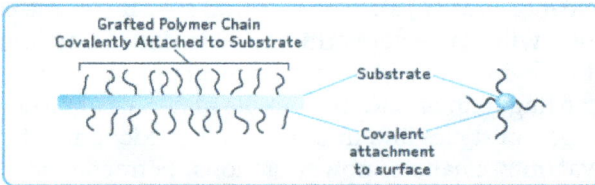

Grafted Polymer Chain Covalently Attached to Substrate

Substrate

Covalent attachment to surface

Similarly, a filter fabric intended to use at the high temperatures may not be a good chemical resistant. The **selection criteria for filters** is based on,

- flow rate/capacity,
- pressure drop required,
- filtration efficiency / micron rating,
- moisture conditions,
- PH value,
- operating temperature,
- type of cleaning system,
- nature of gas / liquid involved

Advantages of Nonwoven Filter

Advantages of nonwoven filter over the woven filters are:

1) High permeability

2) High filtration efficiency

3) Less blinding tendency

4) No yarn slippage as in woven media

5) Good gasketing characteristics

6) Good cake discharge

Principles of Filtration

Filtration, as a physical operation is very important in chemistry for the separation of materials of different chemical composition. Objective of filter medium is to maximize the possibility of collision and the subsequent retention of the suspended particles with fibrous structures while minimizing the energy loss of the system. The efficiency of filtration in industrial fabrics are affected by there porosity. Knowledge of air permeability is also important for suitability for use. Permeability is capacity of porous materials to transmit the fluids. Liquid and gas permeability increases with the increase in porosity of the fabric. The type of finish also affects the permeability. When Porosity increases pressure drop tends to decrease. When flow rate increases, pressure drop increases. There are five principles of filtration which are discussed as below:

Interception: When a particle tries to pass the fibre surface from the distance smaller than the radius of particle, it may collide with the fibre and may be stopped or arrested.

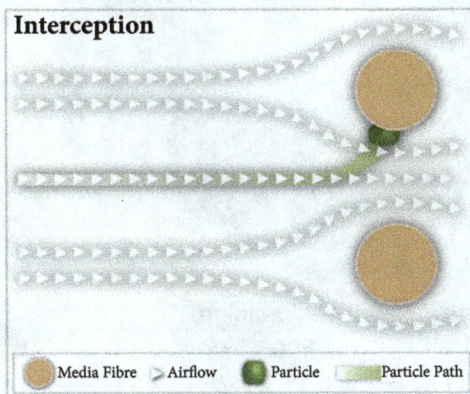

Inertial disposition: When heavy particles are carried in the flow, they may be thrown out from the streamline flow due to its inertia. This may cause the particle to be trapped in the fibres.

Random diffusion (Brownian motion): Due to random vibrations and zigzag movement of particles in the flow, particles may follow zigzag route causing chances of trapping.

Electrostatic disposition: Micro particles are very difficult to capture with mechanical methods. Strong electrostatic charges on the fibres increase filtration efficiency.

Gravitational forces: Under the influence of the gravity, a particle that is sinking may collide with the fibres and get caught.

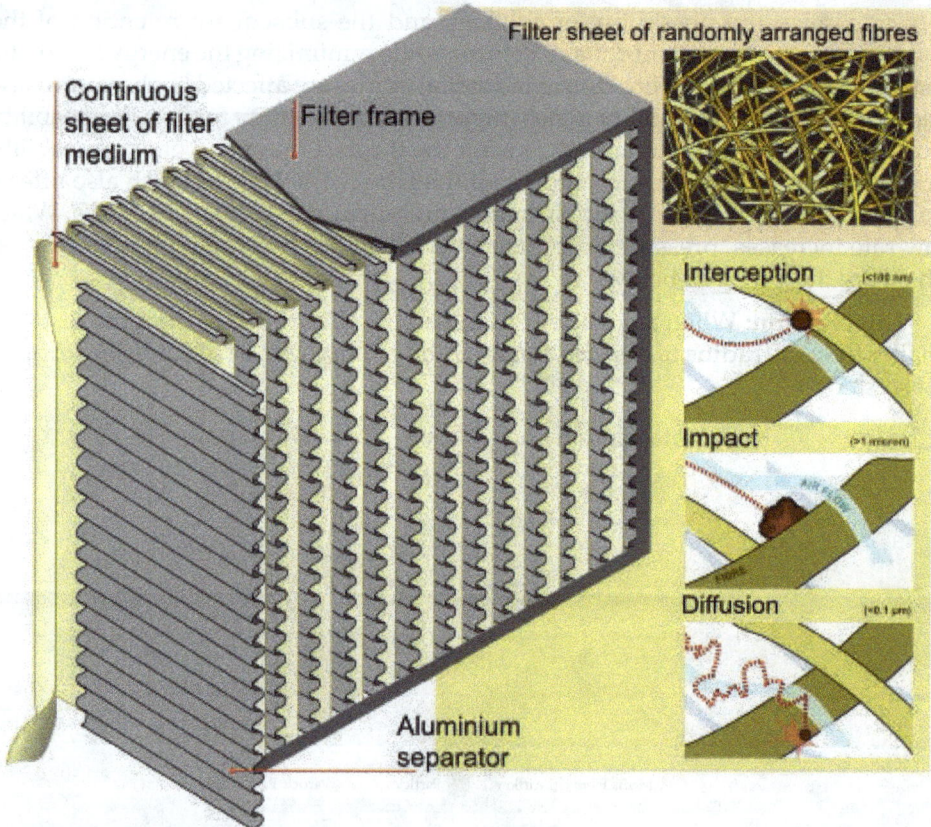

Classification of Filtration

Depending on the process of separation, filtration is classified as:

Reverse osmosis: Reverse osmosis is similar to the membrane filtration treatment process. However, there are key differences between reverse osmosis and filtration. The predominant removal mechanism in membrane filtration is straining, or size exclusion, so the process can theoretically achieve perfect exclusion of particles regardless of operational parameters such as influent pressure and concentration. RO (Reverse Osmosis), however involves a diffusive mechanism so that separation efficiency is dependent on influent solute concentration, pressure and water flux rate. It works by using pressure to force a solution through a membrane, retaining the solute on one side and allowing the pure solvent to pass to the other side. This is the reverse of the normal osmosis process, which is the natural movement of solvent from an area of low solute concentration, through a membrane, to an area of high solute concentration when no external pressure is applied.

Nano-filtration: Nano-filtration is a relatively recent membrane filtration process used most often with low total dissolved solids water such as surface water and fresh groundwater, with the purpose of softening (polyvalent cation removal) and removal of disinfection by-product precursors such as natural organic matter and synthetic organic matter. Nano-filtration is also becoming more widely used in food processing applications such as dairy, for simultaneous concentration and partial (monovalent ion) demineralisation. Nano-filtration (NF) is a cross-flow filtration technology which ranges somewhere between ultra filtration (UF) and reverse osmosis (RO). The nominal pore size of the membrane is typically below 1 nanometer, thus Nano-filtration. Nano-filter membranes are typically rated by molecular weight cut-off (MWCO) rather than nominal pore size. The trans-membrane pressure (pressure drop across the membrane) is required considerably lower than the one used for RO, reducing the operating cost significantly. However, NF membranes are still subject to scaling and fouling and often modifiers such as anti-scalants are required for use.

Ultra filtration: Ultra filtration (UF) is a variety of membrane filtration in which hydrostatic pressure forces a liquid against a semi permeable membrane. Suspended solids and solutes of high molecular weight are retained, while water and low molecular weight solutes pass through the membrane. This separation process is used in industry and research for purifying and concentrating macromolecular solutions, especially protein solutions. Ultra filtration is not fundamentally different from microfiltration or nano-filtration, except in terms of the size of the molecules it retains. Mostly, ultra filtration is applied in cross-flow mode and separation in ultra filtration undergoes concentration polarisation.

Microfiltration: Microfiltration is a filtration process, which removes contaminants from a fluid (liquid & gas) by passage through a micro porous membrane. A typical microfiltration membrane pore size range is 0.1 to 10 microns (μm). Microfiltration is fundamentally different from reverse osmosis and nano-filtration because those systems use pressure as a means of forcing water to go from low pressure to high pressure. Microfiltration can use a pressurised system but it does not need to include pressure.

Particle filtration: Particle filtration is the separation of particles having size above 10 microns. These can be filtered out easily without any usage of micro porous membrane.

Filters

The broad category of filters is classified in two groups, i.e., Dry (air/dust) Filters and Wet Filters. The selection criteria for filters is based on flow rate/capacity, pressure drop required, filtration efficiency / micron rating, moisture conditions, PH value, operating temperature, type of cleaning system, nature of gas / liquid involved etc.

Dry Filtration

Air filtration is used to provide clean air by filtering off dust and other suspended particles. Dust filtration is to prevent dust (usually industrial) to escape outside. These are referred to as Dust Collectors or Pollution Control Filters.

Air Filters

Air filter is a device that cleans air. It removes contaminants such as dust, mold, and bacteria from the air.

- **Mechanical filters** remove dust and particles by capturing them on the filter media.

- **Electro statically charged filter media** in which the fibers of the media are charged increasing filter efficiency.

- **Electronic air cleaners** attract charged particles to oppositely charged collectors.

Air filters are constructed of filter media, sealants, a frame, and sometimes a faceguard and/or gasket.

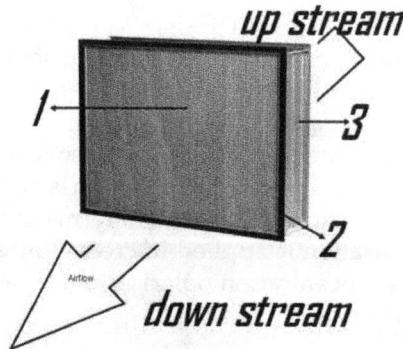

- **Media** is the filtering material. Common types of media include glass fiber, synthetic fiber, non-woven fiber, and PTFE.

- **Sealant** is the adhesive material that creates a leak-proof seal between the filter media and the frame.

- **Frame** is where the filter media is inserted. It can be made from a variety of materials including aluminum, stainless steel, plastic or wood.

- **Faceguard** is a screen attached to the filter to protect the filter media during handling and installation.

- **Gasket** is a rubber or sponge like material used to prevent air leaks between the filter and its housing by compressing the two together.

Air enters the filter through the upstream side. It flows through the filter, contaminants are taken out of the air, and the 'clean' air exits through the downstream side. How 'clean' the air is on the downstream side depends on the efficiency of the filter. Efficiency is the filter's ability to remove particles from the air. Different applications require different levels of efficiency.

Working Principle of Filters (High-Efficiency Particulate Air (Hepa) Filters)

There are three different ways mechanical filters work. They are the straining effect, interception, and diffusion.

Straining Effect: Straining occurs when the particle is bigger than the space between the fibers of the filter media. The particles then collect on the filter media. Straining is only effective with larger particles such as hair or lint.

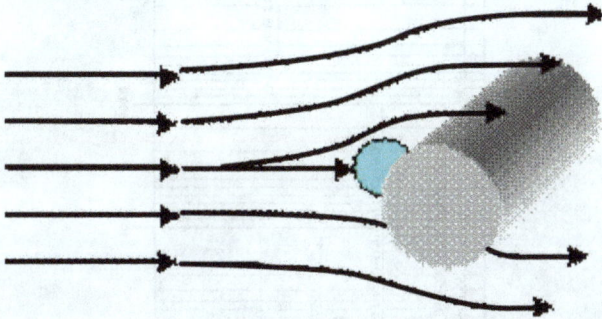

Interception: In this method, particles are small enough to follow the air stream. The particles come in contact with the fibers and remain "stuck" to the fibers because of a weak molecular connection known as Van der Waals' Forces.

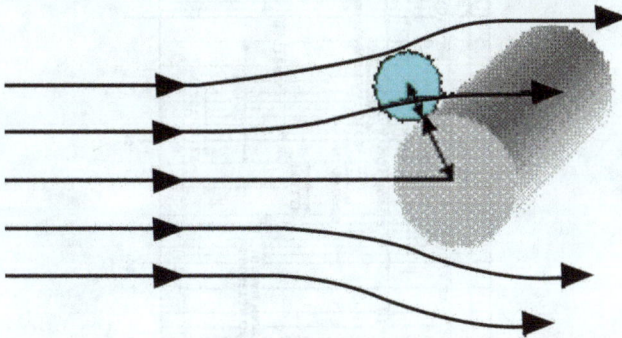

Diffusion: Diffusion works with very small particles and works in HEPA and ULPA filters. The particles are so small that they move in a random motion within the air stream. The random motion causes the particles to stick to the media fibers.

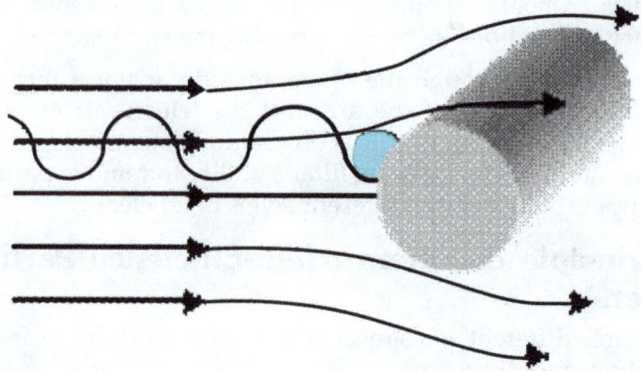

Particle Size

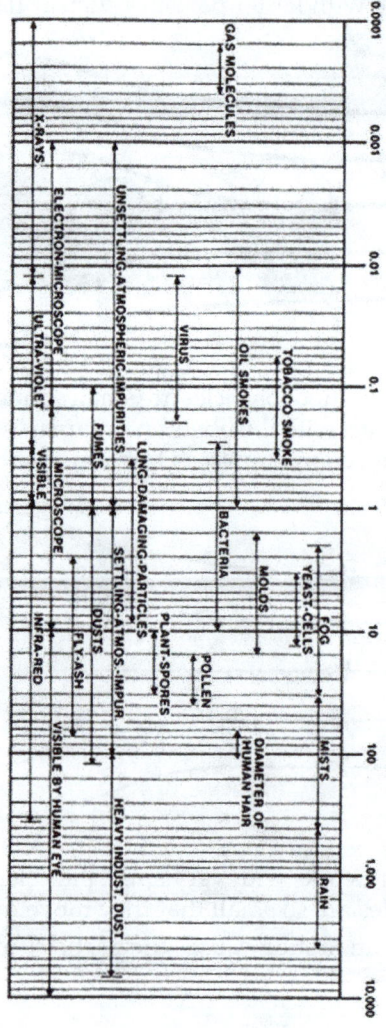

- Human hair   70 – 100 µm
- Human sneeze   10 -100 µm
- Pollen   5 – 100 µm
- Spores   6 – 100 µm
- Mold   2 – 20 µm
- Smoke   0.01 – 1 µm
- Bacteria   0.35 – 10 µm

Air filters are classified in four types based on their efficiency such as,

- Pre-filter (medium efficiency device);
- Fine filter (high efficiency device);
- Super fine filters (dust spot efficiency of high level) and
- HEPA (high efficiency particulate) filters.

High-Efficiency Particulate Air (HEPA) Filters use deeply folded media to trap a minimum of 99.97% of 0.3 micron particles passing through the filter. HEPA filters come in portable, bypass ducted and stand-alone configurations. Beware of manufacturers who use terms like "HEPA-style" or "HEPA-like" filters. Many manufacturers offer HEPA-style filters, but they may only be HEPA at initial efficiencies or by circulating air through the filter numerous times.

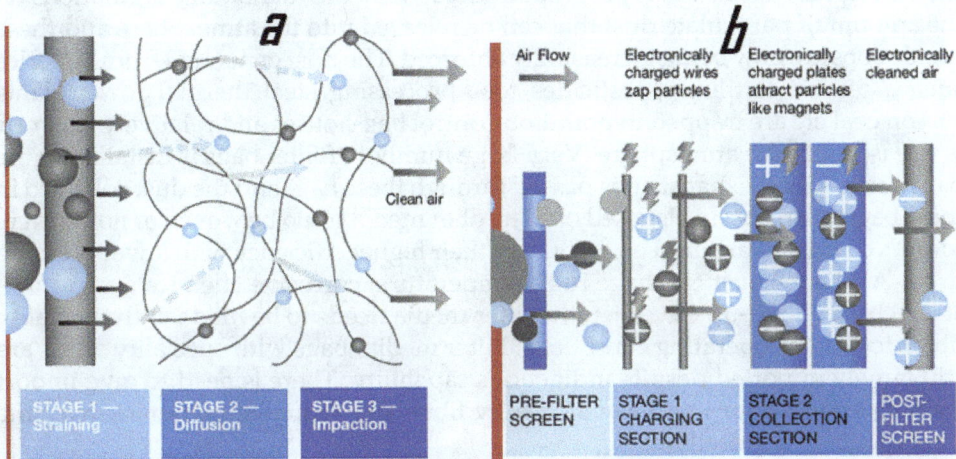

(a) Filter the air using webs of polypropylene fibers to strain, intercept and diffuse airborne particles.

(b) Electrically charge and collect airborne particles on a collection grid. Many electronic air cleaners capture up to 100% of airborne particles passing through the product.

Major Application of Air Filters

Major applications of air filters are as follows:

AREA	FILTER MEDIA
Ventilation and air conditioning systems	non-woven fabric, rubberized coir, glass wool or HEPA Filters
Paint spray booths	synthetic non-woven fabric and also felt, glass wool, wire mesh
Pharmaceutical sectors	synthetic non-woven media, HEPA filters, wire mesh filters, felt filters
Air compressors	wire mesh, paper felt, and synthetic non-woven filter elements
Automobiles	either treated paper or non-woven filter media
Electronic components / products	rubberised coir, wire mesh, glass wool, felt , synthetic non-woven media
Dust collection / pollution control	woven or nonwoven, Filter media/bags with speciality fibres
Bolting cloth	Nylon mono-filament yarn, polyester mono-filament yarn and polyester multi-filament yarn.
Geo filtration	Needle punched nonwoven
Drainage	Jute, thin non-woven, non-woven polypropylene

Dust Collection / Pollution Control

This is one of the most important areas of use of technical textiles and with great potential for growth. Tremendous amount of industrial dust escapes into the atmosphere creating very high pollution. There are mandatory regulations on the amount of particulate dust that can be released into the atmosphere and these regulations are now being increasingly enforced. The dust generated from factories such as cement, fertilizers, pesticides, food processing, steel, thermal power plants run on coal etc are trapped in pollution control bag-houses and relatively clean air is released into the atmosphere. Very large number of filter bags is installed in the bag house. All the exhaust air is passed through these bags and the dust collected in these bags is separately disposed off. The filter media could be woven or nonwoven. More Nonwovens are used on account of their higher efficiency with lower pressure drop. As the exhaust can have high temperature, corrosive chemicals, moisture, static charge build-up etc., often the filter media needs to be made with speciality fibres to suit the operating conditions. Filter media/bags with speciality fibres are still largely imported despite indigenous capability. There is need to give import duty concessions for import of speciality fibres to encourage manufacture of the filter media/bags locally.

Pharmaceutical Sectors (Formulation and Basic Drugs)

Air filters find usage in pharmaceutical units for filtering the air of dust particles, in the spray coating plant, and in the tableting section for powder recovery. In addition, several units, especially those manufacturing antibiotics, etc., have sterile areas, which are generally air-conditioned, and have HEPA filters fitted into the air conditioning system. Pleated panel type of filters using synthetic non-woven media may account for about 50-55 per cent in value terms the rest being HEPA filters, wire mesh filters, felt filters, etc.

Power Generation

The number and type of air filters and the amount of filter media used in gas turbines varies with the size of the gas turbine. The amount of filter material used for air filters varies according to the shape and design of the filter.

Ventilation and air Conditioning Systems

Since air-conditioning systems draw air from the environment they are important areas of air filters. Depending on the end use application the type of filtering media is used which could be non-woven fabric, rubberized coir, glass wool or HEPA Filters.

Paint Spray Booths (automobile and consumer durable products): The air inside the paint shop should be free of dust and other large particulate matters. For these air filters synthetic non-woven fabric is used (and also felt, glass wool, wire mesh etc.).

Automobiles: Engine air in-take filters for automobiles use either treated paper or non-woven filter media. The use of nonwovens is increasing on account of their low pressure drop and high dust bearing capacity.

Air compressors: The air at the intake stage of the compressors has to be filtered to remove dust so as to avoid wear and tear of the compressor chamber components as also to ensure clean outlet air. At the inlet stage of compressor various filters can be used such as cartridge, panel or pocket type (normally cartridge). These filters are made of wire mesh, paper felt, and synthetic non-woven filter elements.

Electronic Components / Products: A variety of materials are used as filter media such as rubberised coir, wire mesh, glass wool, felt as well as synthetic non-woven media in electronic industry.

Wet Filtration

In wet filtration filter cloth finds wide use in industries like sugar, soft drinks, pharmaceuticals, paints dyestuffs, vegetable oils, as well as in engineering industries. The filter media could be woven, nonwoven or even paper type made from cellulose pulp or cotton. Currently mostly woven filter cloth is used. However, use of nonwovens is gradually increasing. Non-woven filters are also are used for coolants and cutting oil filtration in all engineering industries. There are a few manufacturers of filter media in the organized sector. The major manufacturers are Supreme Nonwovens in Nonwovens and Khosla Filters in Wovens.

Drainage

The use of geotextiles in drainage has made significant strides in changing the conventional procedure of using graded filters. Needle-punched nonwoven geotextile is preferred where drainage is the primary functional requirement. The consumption of geotextiles in the world markets has grown at a phenomenal pace in recent years. Synthetic materials constitute 95 per cent of the total consumption and the natural fibres including jute account for only 5 per cent. In India, geotextiles have been selectively used in road and airport flexible pavements and in overlays. In unpaved roads, introducing a very thin non-woven geotextile is found to be of advantage for soft sub grades primarily through separation and partly through reinforcement. The Central Road Research Institute at New Delhi has taken up studies in rural areas of Gujarat and Maharashtra with black soils. Strips of indigenous bitumen coated non-woven geotextiles have been successfully used in Madurai, Ahmadabad and Chandigarh airports in the runways. Their use is believed to have helped in controlling the cracks. Recently non-woven polypropylene geotextiles have been used in the parallel taxi track of Delhi airport over expansion joints, construction joints and crack surfaces while executing a flexible overlay over distressed rigid pavements. Outstanding advantages of geotextiles in drainage are:

- It eliminates the filter sand with the dual media backfill.
- In some cases, it eliminates the need for perforated pipes.
- In situations where only sand backfill is available, it is possible to wrap the drainage pipe with fabric to act as a screening agent. The fabric,
- There by, prevents the sand from entering perforation in the pipe.
- With Geotextiles, trench excavation is considerably reduced.
- Many times the use of geotextiles eliminates the need for trench shoring.

Bolting Cloth

Bolting cloth belongs to the family of industrial woven fabrics, primarily used for screen printing in the textile processing / printing units. Bolting cloth is a commodity product, traditionally manufactured by the industrial fabric producers engaged in items like filter fabric, canvas, tarpaulins etc. Bolting cloth is made of raw materials like nylon mono-filament yarn, polyester mono-filament yarn and polyester multi-filament yarn. The present trend is towards switching over of the technology from screen printing to roller printing. Hence, there may not be any significant increase in the market size of the bolting cloth.

Geo Filtration

The purpose of geotextiles with reference to drainage and filtration is simply to retain soil while allowing the passage of water. When geotextiles are used as drains, the water flow is within the plane of the geotextile itself i.e., they have high lateral permeability. At the same time, geotextiles must possess adequate dimensional stability to retain their thickness under pressure. It has been observed that the life of pavement of highways or air field pavements etc., is greatly influenced by the time for which the water remains under the structural section and its drainage system which is responsible for the removal of free water which is fed directly from the stone base course beneath the structure. Needle punched nonwoven is the preferred geotextile for such applications where primary requirement is filtration.

Different Types of Engineered Filters

- **Germ Defense Filter** - Trap and reduce airborne bacteria, mold spores, and viruses.
- **Pet Allergy Filter** - This filter traps and reduces pet dander and odors.

- **Toxin Absorber Filter** - Eliminate harmful chemical fumes and volatile organic compounds (VOCs) such as formaldehyde and benzene.

- **Odor Remover Filter** - This activated carbon filter traps and eliminates odors from pets, cigarettes and cigars, cooking, and mildew. Absorbing effectiveness to 91%.

Testing of Filters

It is done to measure the filtering capacity of the fabrics, for intended suspension in liquid filtration. Other factors, which need to be considered, include the rate of filter choking, service life of the filter cloth, filtrate purity and cake removal. Efficiency of filter is directly related with the particle size. As the particle size is increased, the efficiency of the filter increases, and vice versa. It is also increased by selection of proper size of fibre, orientation and packing.

Important Test Characteristics Include

1) Permeability

2) Differential pressure

3) Efficiency

4) Strength

5) Chemical resistance

The flow resistance of the produced composite filters is evaluated by means of air permeability measurements. The electro-spun fibres have diameters ranging from about 70 - 500 nm and are interconnected each other to form thin webs that have very small pore size. After the electro-spinning treatment, the air permeability of the filter media decreases 6 - 17 times showing a significant change of flow resistance that can be controlled by the thickness of nano fibres layer and the pore size. Each filter fabric is intended for a specific use in the specific climate under the specific conditions for its optimum output and enhanced efficiency. For coming decades, filter fabric filtration will play a very critical role in our day-to-day life; there is not a single type of fabric used in all the applications. The usage of the filter fabrics varies according to their end use.

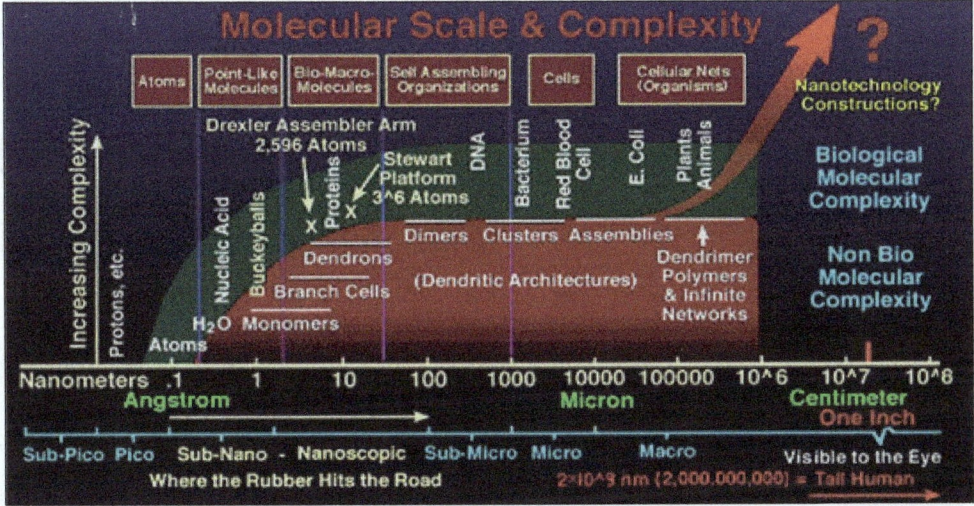

p. 10

Nano-Tex™ Resists Spills Fabric Protection Resist Mud Stains p. 11

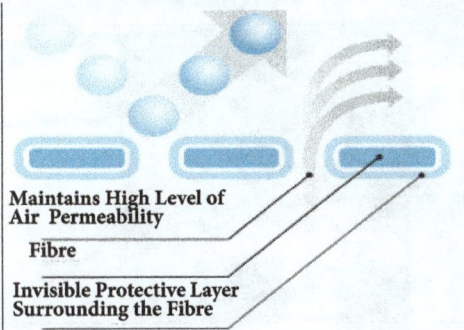

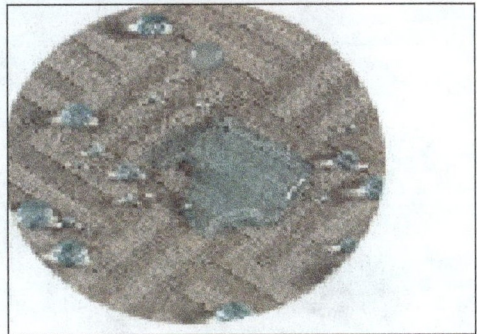

p. 12

p. 12

 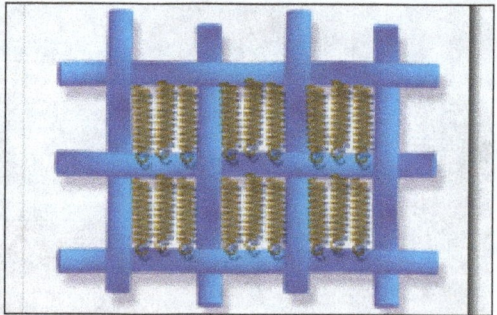

p. 13

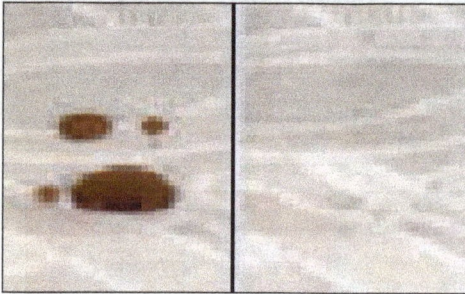 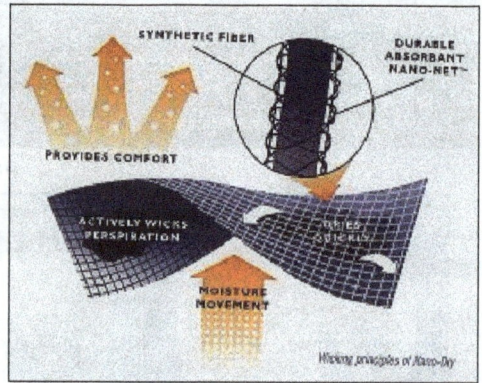

p. 13   p. 14

 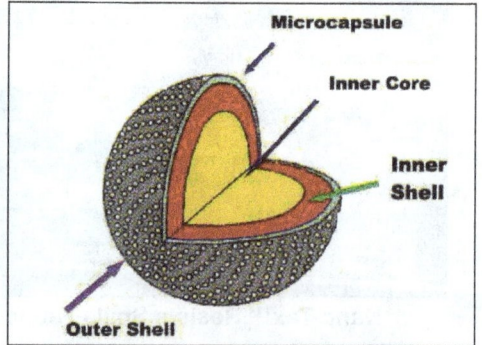

p. 16   p. 19

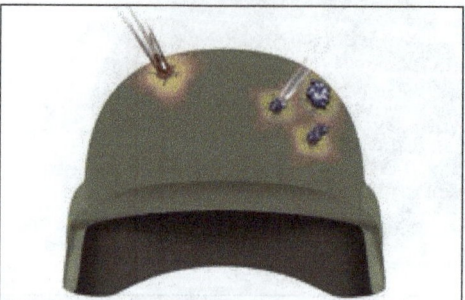 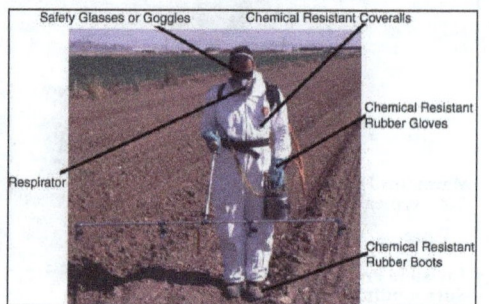

p. 22   p. 23

p. 23

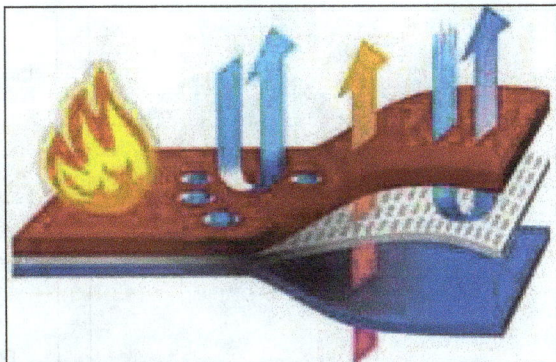

p. 23

p. 25

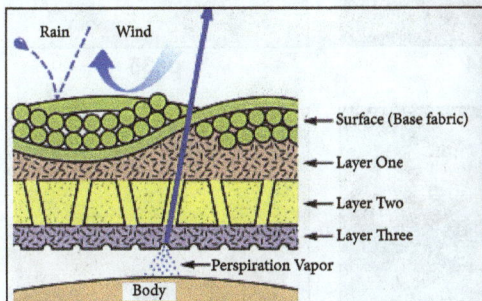

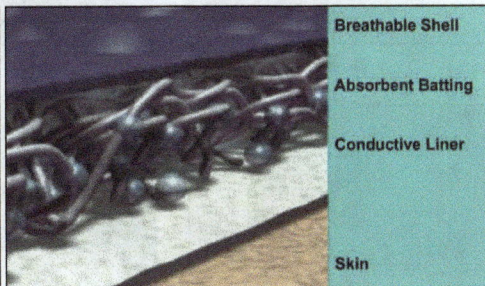

p. 27

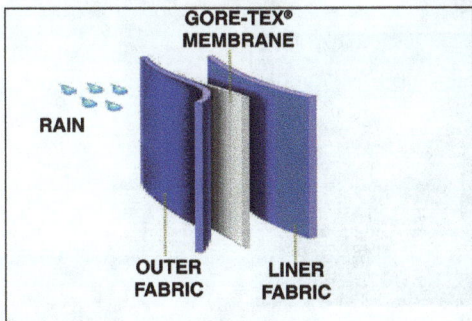

p. 29

p. 30

1. Wind & water completely blocked
2. Outer shell fabric
3. Water vapour molecules pushed outwards
4. Hydrophilic coating

p. 30

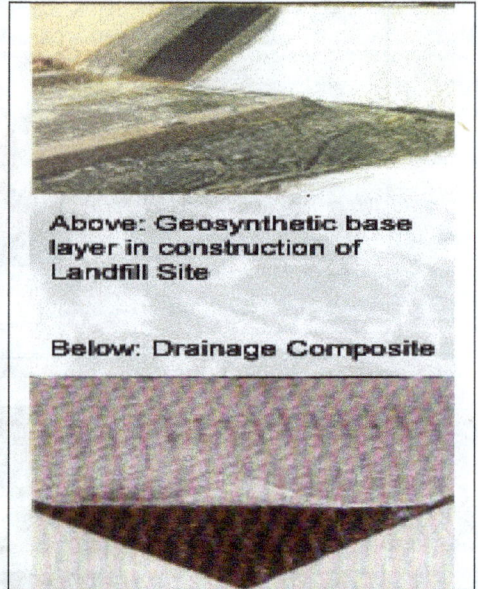

Above: Geosynthetic base layer in construction of Landfill Site

Below: Drainage Composite

p. 33

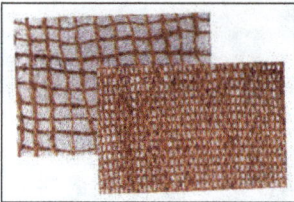

p. 34

p. 34

p. 35

p. 35

p. 42

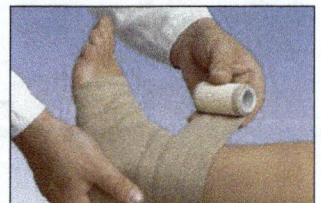

p. 42

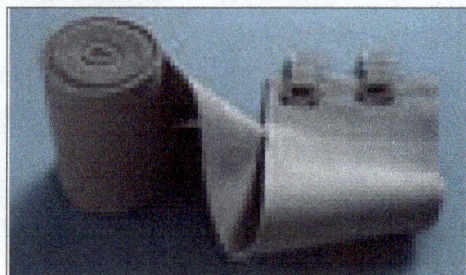

p. 42

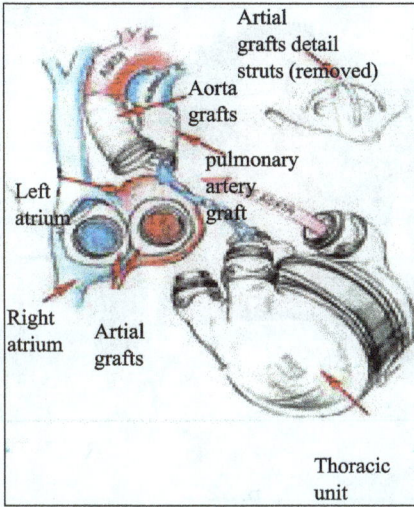

Artial
grafts detail
struts (removed)

Aorta
grafts

pulmonary
artery
graft

Left
atrium

Right
atrium   Artial
grafts

Thoracic
unit

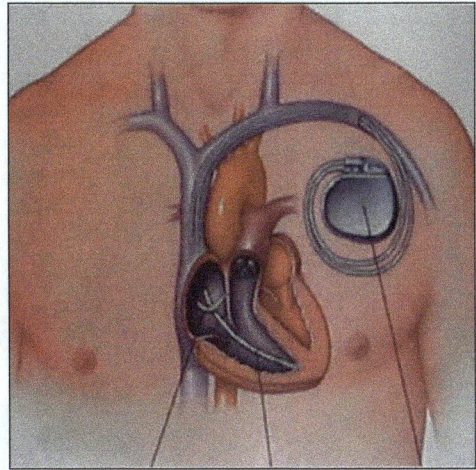

p. 46

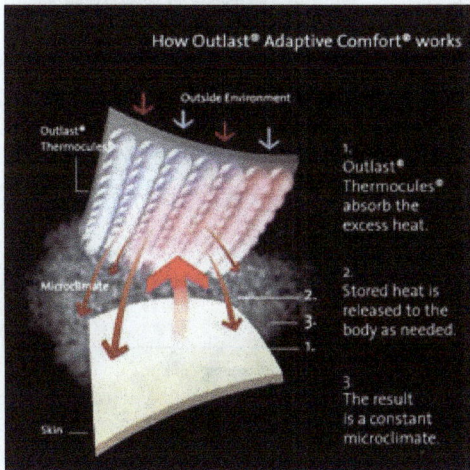

How Outlast® Adaptive Comfort® works

Outside Environment

Outlast®
Thermocules®

1.
Outlast®
Thermocules®
absorb the
excess heat.

Microclimate

2.
Stored heat is
released to the
body as needed.

Skin

3
The result
is a constant
microclimate.

p. 50

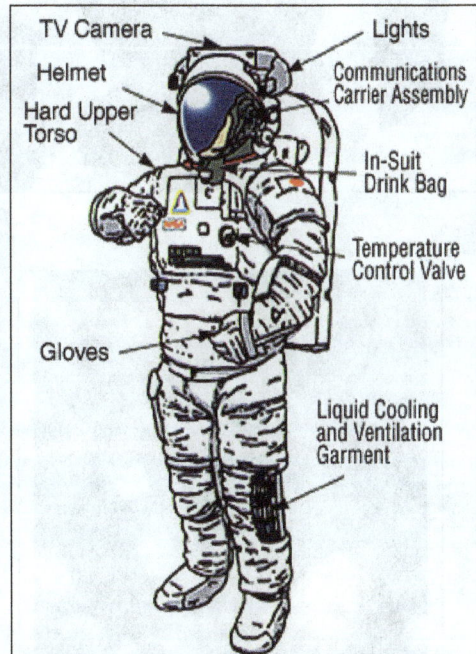

TV Camera   Lights

Helmet   Communications
                                   Carrier Assembly
Hard Upper
Torso

                                   In-Suit
                                   Drink Bag

                                   Temperature
                                   Control Valve

Gloves

                                   Liquid Cooling
                                   and Ventilation
                                   Garment

p. 51

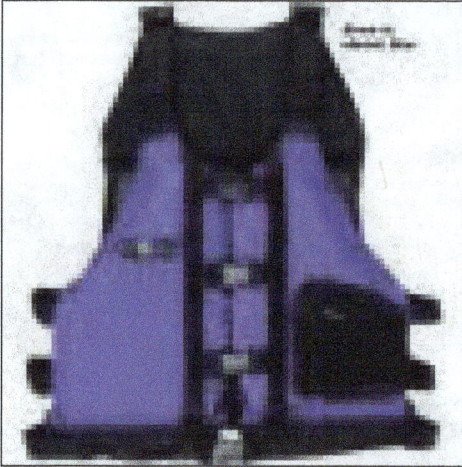

p. 52

p. 52

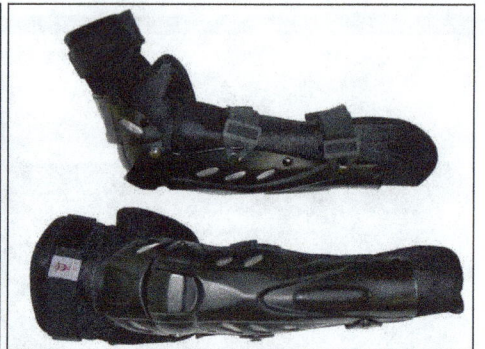

p. 53

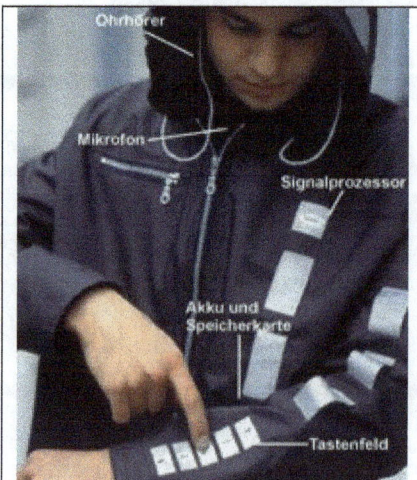

Ohrhörer

Mikrofon

Signalprozessor

Akku und
Speicherkarte

Tastenfeld

p. 54

p. 55

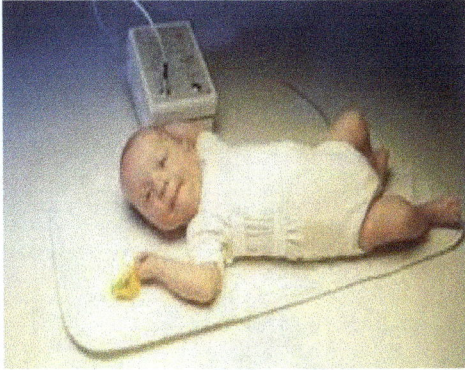

p. 58

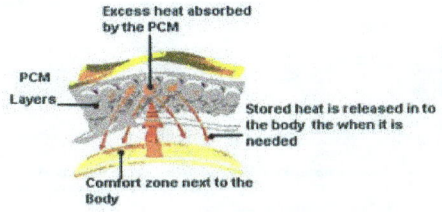

Excess heat absorbed by the PCM

PCM Layers

Stored heat is released in to the body the when it is needed

Comfort zone next to the Body

p. 60

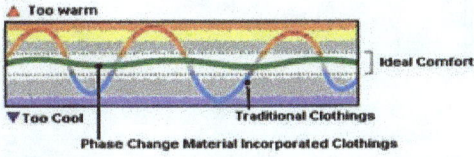

▲ Too warm

Ideal Comfort

▼ Too Cool

Traditional Clothings

Phase Change Material Incorporated Clothings

p. 60

H_2O

H_2O O_2-CO_2 Compostex®

p. 67

p. 68

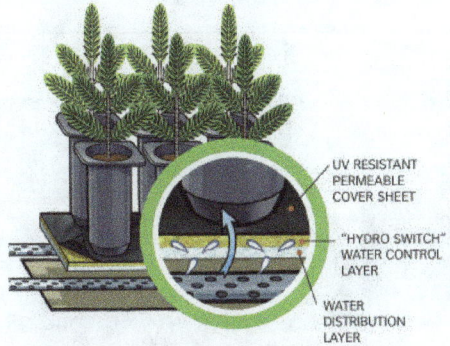

UV RESISTANT PERMEABLE COVER SHEET

"HYDRO SWITCH" WATER CONTROL LAYER

WATER DISTRIBUTION LAYER

p. 69

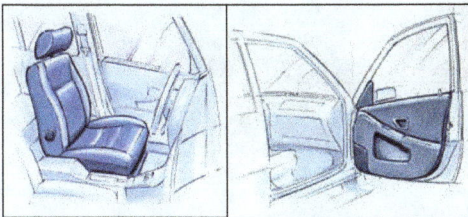

p. 76

p. 77

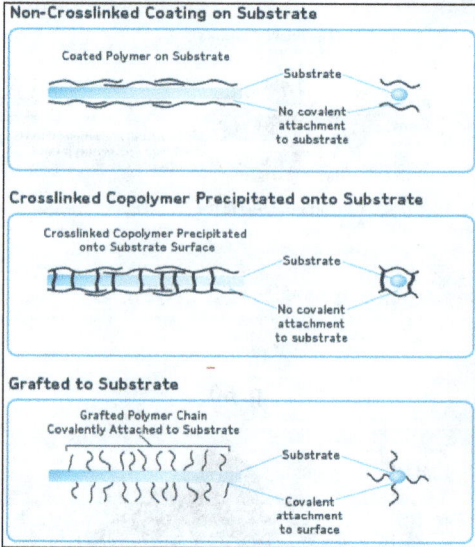

p. 80

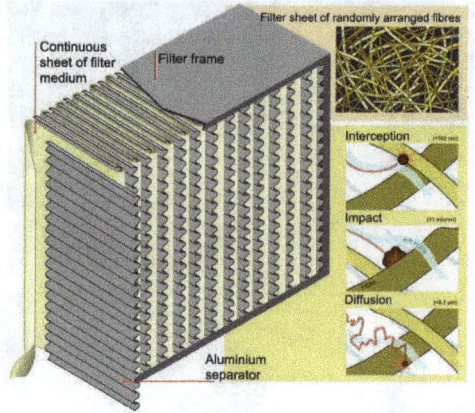

p. 82

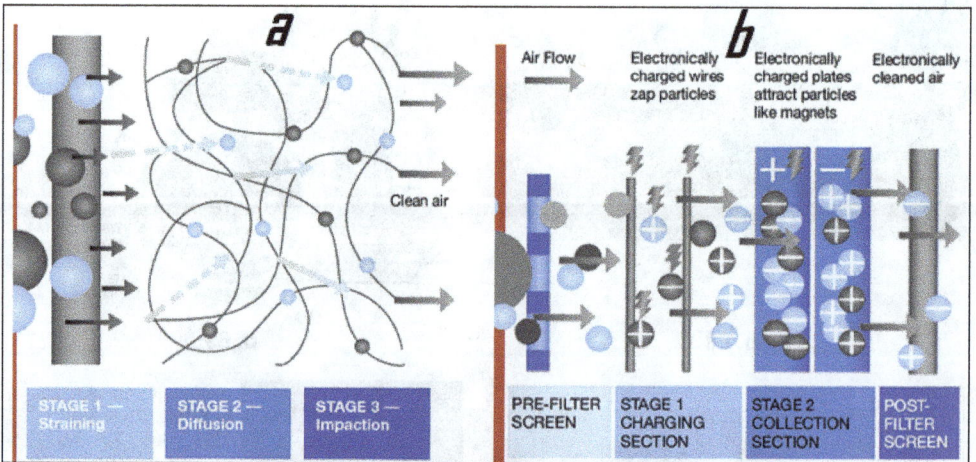

p. 87

www.ingramcontent.com/pod-product-compliance
Lightning Source LLC
Chambersburg PA
CBHW050227270326
41914CB00003BA/597

9 789388 173728